Qatar-USA
A Half-Century Journey

Khalid Al-Jaber & Patrick Theros

Table of Contents

Introduction: A Half-Century of Qatar-U.S. Ties. 5

Chapter 1: A Brief History of Qatar 17

Chapter 2: The Early Days of the Qatar-U.S. Relationship 35

Chapter 3: From Pearl Diving to the Global Economy. 53

Chapter 4: Domestic Governance: From Traditional to Modern. . 71

Chapter 5: A Small State with a Global Influence 89

Chapter 6: The Evolution of Qatar's Education System. 109

Chapter 7: Qatar Becomes a Leader in International Media 127

Chapter 8: Doha's Soft Power: Culture, Art, and Museums 145

Chapter 9: The Sports Hub of the Middle East 161

Chapter 10: The Qatari-American Strategic Partnership 177

Conclusion. 195

Bibliography. 201

About the Authors 213

Copyright © 2021 MENA Center

All rights reserved. No part of this publication may be reproduced, copied or distributed in any form or by any means, or stored in any database or retrieval system, without the express prior written permission of MENA Center. No part of this publication shall be reproduced, modified, transmitted, distributed, disseminated, sold, published, sub-licensed, or have derivative work created or based upon it, without the express prior written permission of MENA Center. If you wish to reproduce any part of this publication, please contact MENA Center.

MENA Center
1717 K St NW, Washington, DC 20005

Printed in the United States of America.

ISBN: 978-1-7328043-8-8

MENA Center does not take institutional positions on public policy issues; the views represented herein are the authors' own and do not necessarily reflect the views of MENA Center, its staff, or board members. All materials found in this publication have been prepared for informational purposes only. The information herein is provided without any representations or warranties, express or implied, regarding the com pleteness, accuracy, reliability, suitability or availability with respect to the publication or the information, products, services, or related graphics contained in the publication for any purpose. In no event will MENA Center be liable for any loss or damage including without limitation, indirect or consequential loss or damage, or any loss or damage whatsoever arising from loss of data or profits arising out of, or in connection with, the use of this publication.

Introduction
A Half-Century of Qatar-U.S. Ties

The United States and Qatar have developed a deep political, economic, and societal relationship. Qatar has become an indispensable hub for the American military presence in the Middle East, the Arabian Peninsula, and the Indian Ocean. This region is home to two-thirds of the world's proven oil reserves and half of the world's natural gas, and by protecting the free flow of energy through the Gulf, the United States helps to maintain an integral pillar of the world economy, which serves America's economic interests. Even though comparatively little of this oil and gas is directly exported to the United States, the U.S. economy depends greatly on a well-functioning world economy and a high level of international trade.

America's ability to maintain its position in the Middle East is greatly facilitated by its relationship with Qatar. Moreover, Qatar has dedicated itself to the pursuit of such universal values as human rights and education. Though these values are often derided in the region as "Western values," many Qatari people understand them as universal values that they share with Americans.

The Qatari-American relationship has long been underpinned by political and trade links and friendly cooperation between the Qatari and American people. If the relationship is to endure, it will be because Americans understand the necessity of a positive relationship with Qatar, and vice versa. All Americans have a civic responsibility to know what the United States is doing in the Gulf, considering the region's vital importance, and should be able to see beyond news reporting about wars and disasters to truly understand the region and our shared interests. The authors of this book—one a Qatari academic, one a former U.S. ambassador—

Introduction

wrote it with the intention of providing a deeper understanding of the relationship between two such dissimilar countries to a broad audience. The Qatari-American relationship officially began fifty years ago, although initial contacts preceded official recognition by almost another fifty years. In the history of relationships between countries, this one has been comparatively brief.

Many books have been written quite recently about Qatar, but few, if any, have addressed the full history and spectrum of the U.S. relationship with Qatar. Our purpose in this publication is to focus on the contacts between Qatar and the United States over time and the ways the two societies have influenced one another. Like all relationships, there have been differences and disagreements, and this will almost certainly happen again in the future. Other countries have differing views on the Gulf's future, and tensions and disagreements are inevitable. Therefore, we hope that readers will come away equipped with the knowledge to understand these future tensions.

The Gulf region, including Qatar, first became important to the developed world—and particularly to the United States—after the first discoveries of oil in the region in the early 1900s, although the value of oil prior to the Second World War remained very low by modern standards. However, even during its period of international isolation, America clearly knew of Qatar's existence and sought to cultivate links to it—to the frustration of the region's suzerain, the United Kingdom, which had signed protection agreements with the small Gulf states during that era. British officials stationed in Qatar during the 1930s, particularly those affiliated with the Anglo-Iranian Oil Company (later British Petroleum), warned London that American oilmen had an unusual interest in developing ties to Qatar—ties that the British did their best to prevent, although American firms soon secured minority stakes in the regional oil company. American ties in Qatar expanded in other ways as well, notably with the creation of a new hospital by the American Mission in Bahrain, a group of Christian missionaries whose charitable work provided some of the earliest contacts between Americans and the people of the Gulf.

In 1971, with the withdrawal of the British, Qatar gained its independence. Though the following decade was one of great regional upheaval, it was also a time of great prosperity. The pearl-diving

Introduction

economy within Qatar had collapsed earlier in the century due to competition from Asia, but the nation soon discovered a new source of wealth—oil—and, after petroleum prices dramatically increased during the 1970s, gained fantastic wealth. Qatar experienced a second windfall in the 1990s when development of its natural gas reserves made it the richest nation per capita in the world. With its immense wealth, Qatar soon began to develop as a modern state.

Qatar quickly sought to raise its profile on the international stage and develop a reputation as a modern state. To this end, it immediately embarked on ambitious development programs—in many cases using the United States as a model for emulation, for instance in the development of its education system and its journalistic institutions. However, although mineral wealth helped to sustain economic development, Qatar's leaders knew that it was a small state in a troubled region, and that the nation's continued stability and well-being depended on good relations with larger powers. One of the first nations with which Qatar sought to build ties was the United States, and America was happy to reciprocate. Within a year, the United States recognized the small state's independence and began construction in 1973 of an embassy in Doha, Qatar's capital.

Qatari-American relations were established at a uniquely opportune time. During the 1970s, the Gulf region became increasingly important to America's national strategic calculation. The region was the source of one-third of the world's oil, a commodity that the United States continued to import at an ever-increasing rate. The region was also rocked by instability; during the 1970s, it experienced two massive oil shocks and an earth-shaking revolution in Iran. In response to these events, and to perceived Soviet encroachment in the area, President Jimmy Carter promulgated the "Carter Doctrine:" the idea that any attack on the freedom of commerce in the Gulf would be considered an attack on America's vital interests—an idea that remains central to American defense planning to the current day.

Relations between Qatar and the United States continued to expand throughout the 1970s and 1980s. There were occasional hiccups, such as when Qatar obtained Stinger missiles that the United States had provided to Afghan mujahideen opposing the

Introduction

Soviet Union. Despite this setback, Qatari-American relations dramatically improved again in 1991, when Qatar played a small but important role in the liberation of Kuwait from Saddam Hussein's Iraq. America's victory in the Gulf War paved the way for a 1992 Defense Cooperation Agreement between the two countries.

After a few years, the relationship became even more important when construction began in Qatar on the Al Udeid Air Base, where more than ten thousand American soldiers are currently stationed. Al Udeid later played a critical role in the fight against ISIS and today is the hub of America's operations in the Middle East. Now, nearly fifty years after Qatar's independence, the United States and Qatar are the closest they have ever been; billions of dollars are mutually invested between the two countries each year, and an estimated forty thousand Americans live and work in Qatar.

Qatar is a modern state in every sense. Its leadership, though a monarchy, exercises its decisions by consensus and with input from its advisory Shura Council. In 2003, a constitution limiting the monarch's power and outlining the rights of the people was created and approved by a referendum, with 98 percent of Qataris in support. Elections to Qatar's Municipal Council have already taken place several times, and the first elections to its Shura Council took place in October of 2021.

Qatar has a rich tradition of education. In the past, many regional leaders were educated at Qatari institutions, and the people of Qatar have long understood the importance of learning. However, following Qatar's independence, the nation has paid particular attention to the American model of university education and has attempted to emulate it.

Efforts to reproduce America's education model within Qatar, which have continued for more than twenty years, were particularly pronounced under Emir Sheikh Hamad (r. 1995-2013), who spearheaded Doha's Education City complex. Today, thousands of Qatari students attend school in the United States, and thousands more study at the half-dozen American universities, which have—at the express invitation of the emir—established satellite campuses in Education City. Qatar has also modernized Qatar University, a major domestic university of its own.

Introduction

Qatar has also established an ambitious sports program. Its leaders have understood that sport, although ostensibly apolitical, has clear political and economic importance to participating nations and can provide both entertainment and social cohesion. For this reason, Qatar has undertaken an elaborate program to improve the nation's sports program throughout the twenty-first century.

This effort reached its zenith in 2010 when Qatar was selected—over the far larger and heavily favored United States—to host the 2022 FIFA World Cup. Although preparing to host the World Cup is an extremely difficult task, Qatar rose admirably to the challenge. Moreover, when Qatar's construction program drew the attention of the international press to the plight of mistreated foreign workers throughout the Middle East, the country took serious steps to improve their conditions.

While Qatar has established itself as a modern state, it still maintains a deep connection to its historic past. To this end, Qatar has funded significant cultural and social programs, including museums, archaeological sites, and cultural institutions such as the Katara Cultural Village Foundation. This has bolstered a greater sense of Qatar's history, and hence its people's sense of nationhood; it has also encouraged a greater understanding of the past, both among Qataris and an international audience.

Qatar's fearless encouragement of journalism has set the trend for the rest of the Middle East. It has taken the idea of "freedom of the press," as expressed in the U.S. Constitution's First Amendment, to heart; it is the only country in the region that does not have an official censorship office, and it explicitly gives Qataris the right to work as journalists, rather than permitting them to do so if they meet certain qualifications.

Today, Qatar has a number of popular and widely-circulated newspapers in both Arabic and English that are read throughout the Arab world. Qatar is also notable as the home of the internationally-acclaimed Al Jazeera Channel, which became the first major Arab television channel to achieve regional and worldwide success after the advent of satellite broadcasting. Al Jazeera became one of the first outlets in the Middle East to cover the news for the sake of journalism

Introduction

rather than to advance a governmental viewpoint. It also covered issues objectively, with the slogan, "The Opinion and the Other Opinion." This framework gave it a massive advantage over its competitors, which, for political reasons, were constrained in their reporting.

Al Jazeera played a critical role in the democratic uprisings of the 2011 Arab Spring. While the government-run outlets avoided covering the protests to appease their leaders, Al Jazeera covered them comprehensively; the network's correspondents were often the only media professionals in Tahrir Square during the Egyptian Revolution. Al Jazeera's fact-based, accurate coverage of the events helped to mobilize protesters and earned it praise from many other countries, including the United States, where Secretary of State Hillary Clinton praised the network in Congressional testimony. However, this reporting earned it the enmity of several of its neighbors, and Qatar's open support for the Arab Spring revolutions was one of the major causes of a 2014 diplomatic crisis between Qatar and Bahrain, Saudi Arabia, and the United Arab Emirates.

Although the 2014 crisis was soon resolved, a similar crisis erupted in 2017 when the same three nations—now joined by Egypt—embargoed Qatar and issued a thirteen-point ultimatum that included the closure of Al Jazeera as a condition for lifting it. Qatar, which had no intention of acceding to the demands, relied on its international partnerships for support. During the crisis, Qatar's close friendship with the United States became apparent. While President Donald Trump initially took the side of Saudi Arabia and the United Arab Emirates and criticized Qatar, he later moderated his views and insisted on a peaceful diplomatic end to the crisis. In April 2018, Trump also welcomed Qatar's emir, Sheikh Tamim, to the Oval Office, a powerful symbolic gesture of support. President Trump and his envoy Jared Kushner were essential to bringing the crisis to an end in January 2021.

Finally, Qatar, by virtue of its friendship with both the United States and conservative Islamist groups that America opposes, has been able to act as a mediator in regional conflicts. Its position as a conservative Muslim country has allowed it to make inroads where the United States could not. Qatar has served as a mediator in several key conflicts, including in Lebanon, Sudan, and Palestine, where it negotiated a 2007 settlement between main

Palestinian factions Fatah and Hamas. Most prominently, Qatar has served as the chief mediator between the United States and the Taliban in Afghanistan. Qatar negotiated a prisoner exchange between the two parties in 2014, exchanging Sgt. Bowe Bergdahl for five Taliban prisoners held in Guantanamo Bay. It also hosted the 2019 peace talks between America and the Taliban, resulting in a peace agreement that continues to be implemented.

 Taken together, all of this illustrates the priorities that Qatar's leadership has set for the young nation. While rich, Qatar is not powerful in a military sense; it is a small nation that depends heavily on regional peace and security and the existence of a stable international order. That order has historically been guaranteed by the United States, and Qatar has sought to maintain it by supporting America's mission in the Middle East. Although the two countries will have their differences, as all nations do, the United States and Qatar have a mutually beneficial relationship, and the political and commercial ties between the two will continue to advance. The following paragraphs provide an overview of the layout of *Qatar-USA: A Half-Century Journey.*

 The second chapter of *Qatar-USA: A Half-Century Journey* details the history of Qatar's relationship with the United States, its most important security partner. Qatar-U.S. ties predate Qatari statehood by nearly a half-century. In 1934, American oil companies made contact with Qataris in Doha in search of new oil deposits as part of Washington's policy of "active oil diplomacy." Of course, America faced stiff opposition to encroachment from the dominant regional powers during this period—France and Great Britain. During the protectorate period, American engagement with Qatar flowed through several American oil companies that operated in the Gulf. During World War Two, Washington's focus turned to Saudi Arabia, which the U.S. saw as a reliable security partner and source of oil. Geopolitical developments in the 1950s and 1960s would bring Qatar and the U.S. together, however. After the the promuglation of the anti-communist Eisenhower Doctrine, the failed Suez Crisis of 1956, and the American intervention in Lebanon in 1958, the U.S. found itself deeply involved in the Arab world. After the withdrawal of British forces "east of the Suez" in 1968, the U.S. stepped into the Gulf and replaced Great Britain as the principal security guarantor of

Introduction

the Gulf monarchies, including Qatar. On September 1, 1971, Qatar declared its independence. Three days later, the U.S. recognized Qatar, and the modern Qatar-U.S. relationship was born.

Before the 20th century, Qatar was little more than a collection of villages, its economy almost entirely dependent on pearl diving and transiting traders. Today, Qatar boasts the highest GDP per capita in the world, an increasingly diversified economy, and a highly educated population. Chapter three details the immense transformation Qatar has undergone since the protectorate era. The wealth the small country enjoys today was not always guaranteed. In fact, the pearl industry collapsed in the 1920s after competition from Japan and the Great Depression depressed the global market. After oil was discovered in 1939, Qatar signed agreements with foreign oil companies to extract this increasingly valuable and lucrative resource. Production began in 1949, and oil fundamentally changed the Qatari state. Villages that used to produce pearls suddenly found themselves working in the oil sector, and Qatari nomads quit their traditional way of life to pursue greater riches in fledgling cities. The growing exploitation of natural gas resources in the mid-1990s and the prescient decision of the Qatari government to invest in early liquified natural gas (LNG) cemented Qatar's economic growth in the short- and medium-term, and continues to fuel strategic investments made by the Qatar Investment Authority, the country's sovereign wealth fund.

Chapter four deals with the topic of domestic governance in Qatar. In this sense, Qatar is unlike the other Gulf monarchies, which maintain a firm grip over their societies. Doha has introduced reforms that allow democratic selection of members of the Consultative Assembly, or Shura Council. Qatar also demonstrated a strong willingness to respond to international criticism when it overhauled its labor laws after condemnation from human rights groups. Doha has pursued economic and governance reforms that would grant younger generations greater say in government, and women enjoy full suffrage rights. Two women, including the deputy speaker, serve on the Shura Council. Most notably, the judiciary in Qatar is independent from the ruling family, and state interference in press freedom is minimal. Although Qatar remains a monarchy and the

Emir holds significant power, the state has handed some power back to the citizenry in the 21st century. Qatar's evolution reflects a tendency to respond to the concerns of the governed—a phenomenon all too rare in other Gulf monarchies. This can be put down to the unique historical experiences of Qatari sovereigns. Qatari rulers relied on tax revenue and annual levies on the various tribes—a haphazard and often tense method of governing. The discovery and exploitation of oil and natural gas cemented the central ruler as the focal point of government in Qatar. Despite this, Qatar has sought to empower women, youth, and other historically marginalized communities in its quest for more effective and equitable governance.

The fifth chapter examines the evolution of Qatar-U.S. security and diplomatic ties. Qatar is a small country by most metrics, and does not possess powerful military forces. Despite this, Doha has leveraged its culture of deft diplomacy, its relationship with the United States, and its immense wealth to maximize its influence in the Gulf region and beyond. After the 1991 Gulf War, Qatar and the United States signed a formal defense agreement, which gave U.S. forces basing rights in the country. Washington's largest forward operating base, the Al Udeid air base outside of Doha, soothes Qatar's desire for greater security and serves the American military's need for a secure platform to exert influence throughout the region. The mutually beneficial security relationship between Qatar and the U.S. is rooted in the Nixon Doctrine, which identified Iran and Saudi Arabia as key actors in Gulf security (and thus U.S. access to Middle East hydrocarbon resources). The tumult of the 1970s that culminated the overthrow of the Shah in 1979 only underscored the region's importance to the U.S. Qatar hosts the headquarters of the U.S. Central Command, and has won the support of American politicians from both parties. During the 2017 diplomatic schism between Qatar and other GCC and Arab states, the U.S. Congress consistently supported a swift resolution to the crisis. Qatar is more than a staging area for American troops, however; it is also a trusted diplomatic partner whose ability to liaise between U.S. negotiators and adversaries has proved essential to ending the war in Afghanistan. On January 31, 2022, in light of its efforts in Afghanistan, President Biden designated Qatar a "major non-NATO ally," clearing the way for future security cooperation.

Introduction

The foundation of any society is its youth, and Qatar has taken great strides to enhance its education sector as part of its Vision 2030 program. Chapter six addresses this pillar of societal development. Qatar, like many of the Gulf monarchies, has made great strides in this regard. The first primary and secondary schools on the peninsula opened in the 1950s and 1960s. Tertiary education during the colonial immediate post-colonial period was unavailable to all but the most wealthy Qataris who could afford to send their children overseas. As is the case with much of Qatar's post-colonial development, advancements in the education sector have come through partnership with the United States. Several elite American universities now host campuses in Qatar. Another significant shift has benefitted the education of Qatari youth—the shift from state-run schools to universal schooling independent of government censorship and oversight. This "Independent School System" was first implemented in 2004, and since 2010 all primary and secondary schools operate separately from the state. Enabling freedom of thought enhances the country's prospects for economic dynamism and furthers the goals of Vision 2030.

The seventh chapter demonstrates how Qatar developed into a global leader in the realm of international media production and consumption. The first indigenous Qatari publications—mainly newspapers and magazines—emerged in the 1950s and 1960s, prior to the state's independence from Great Britain. The first private daily newspaper, Al-Arab, was published in 1972. Qatar has always adapted to the latest developments in telecommunications, and the Qatari press utilized radio and television broadcasts to reach an increasingly engaged audience. The country's flagship Al-Jazeera network, launched in 1996, rivals American and British media companies in its size and the depth and sophistication of its reporting. Al-Jazeera has covered controversial topics—including the 2000 Palestinian Intifada, the 2001 U.S. invasion of Afghanistan and the 2003 invasion of Iraq, and the 2011 Arab Spring—with an independent and professional streak. Although Qatar has faced severe reactions from regional states because of its support for Al-Jazeera, its commitment to covering international events has not wavered. With the emergence of the internet, Qatar has broadened its outreach to international audiences. Qataris themselves are highly connected; over 95 percent of Qataris regularly use the internet, and internet penetration rates continue to climb. The time citizens spend on the internet has also grown. From 2013 to 2017, internet usage among Qataris grew from roughly 37 hours per week to nearly 45—the highest in the region. This marked growth signifies an increasingly connected and digitized Qatari society.

Due to regional instability, artists in the Middle East have fled the traditional cultural centers of Baghdad, Cairo, Beirut, and Damascus for the Gulf states. As chapter eight demonstrates, Qatar's unique history as a crossroads for international travel and relatively open society has attracted artists and fostered a growing artistic scene in the country. Taking note of the United States' effective use of soft power, Qatar has sought to expand its international appeal in recent years. Qatar now hosts numerous archaeological, cultural, Islamic, and art museums, and the government has made significant investments to foster innovation and creativity. Doha, once a settlement that exclusively dealt in the fishing and pearl industries, has transformed into an architectural masterpiece, attracting talent from across the globe to the city. Qatar has leveraged these developments to form cultural exchanges with other states, including the U.S. In September, 2020, Washington and Doha marked 2021 as the Qatar-USA Year of Culture to facilitate intercultural dialogue and exchange. Indeed, as a sign of the close bilateral relationship between the two countries, the U.S. was the guest of honor at the 2022 Doha Book Fair, an initiative that brings literature from all around the world to Qatar's shores. When the world casts its eyes to Qatar for the FIFA World Cup in 2022, the country's cultural tolerance and diversity will be on full display.

Chapter nine demonstrates how Qatar has sought to mimic the U.S.' professional sports model to develop its economy, draw tourists to the country, and bolster its soft power. Indeed, as Qatar's international profile has grown, so have its ambitions to make a name for itself in the world of sports. In 2006, Qatar hosted the Asian Games, demonstrating its commitment to athletic competition and, more importantly, its ability to host weeks-long tournaments. The Qatari government firmly believes in the power of sports to bridge political divides and sees its patronage of Qatari sports leagues as a

Introduction

pillar of its Vision 2030 project. The country's winning bid to host the 2022 FIFA World Cup is particularly remarkable considering Qatar's first official participation in other international competitions took place at the 1984 Summer Olympics. At the Los Angeles games, only 27 male athletes from Qatar took part. The country's preparations for the 2022 World Cup have been fraught with controversy. Reports detailing poor working conditions for migrant workers tasked with building the stadiums resulted in widespread labor law reforms, and international criticism drove the Qatari government to improve the country's human rights record. The government has also made significant efforts to improve the health of its citizenry through strategic investments in sports facilities like the Doha Sports City and the naming of a "National Sports Day."

The tenth and final chapter addresses the historical context, current state, and future of the Qatar-U.S. strategic relationship. This valuable partnership has proved mutually beneficial to both parties, and has fostered security in the Gulf region and greater Middle East since the 1991 Gulf War. That said, deep Qatar-U.S. relations are a relatively new phenomenon—Qatar only recently opened its embassy in Washington two decades ago. Since then, financial, commercial, cultural, and security ties between the two countries have developed greatly. The U.S.-Qatar Business Council and the Qatar America Institute for Culture lay the foundation for greater business cooperation and cultural exchange. Strategic investments from the Qatar Investment Authority have boosted the American economy, and Qatar has generously given to American charities dedicated to supporting youth and children with autism. Across almost every sector, Qatar and the U.S. enjoy a deep, symbiotic relationship. As transformations in the Gulf's international environment continue to shape state behavior, the U.S.-Qatar appears poised to become increasingly important in the years to come.

The Authors

Chapter 1
A Brief History of Qatar

1.1. Introduction

While rich, Qatar is not powerful in a military sense; it is a small nation that depends heavily on regional peace and security and the existence of a stable international order. That order has historically been guaranteed by the United States, and Qatar has sought to maintain it by supporting America's mission in the Middle East. Although the two countries will have their differences, as all nations do, the United States and Qatar have a mutually beneficial relationship, and the political and commercial ties between the two will continue to advance.

Qatar has been famous since ancient times for pearl diving, a profession that has long been linked to the geography and history of the Gulf region and the Arabian Peninsula. Today, the Qatari people enjoy the highest per capita gross domestic product in the world. Qatar has emerged as one of the most important natural gas producers in the world and dominates the global LNG market. The United States is the largest foreign investor in Qatar, an investment that has brought great returns to the American economy.

Qatar has taken leadership positions throughout the Gulf and the Arabian Peninsula and beyond. Through its diplomatic efforts, and often working in partnership with the United States, Qatar has sought to mediate directly to end many regional and international conflicts and disputes.

Chapter 1: A Brief History of Qatar

Geographically, Qatar is a peninsula located on the western coast of the Arabian Gulf. It occupies an area of 11,521 square kilometers, slightly smaller in area than the U.S. state of Connecticut. The Qatari peninsula is about 100 miles (160 km) from north to south, 50 miles (80 km) from east to west, and is roughly ovular in shape. It shares a land border with Saudi Arabia and sea borders with Bahrain, the United Arab Emirates, and Iran.

Qatar first emerged as an independent political entity under the Al Thani dynasty in 1825—well after the establishment of other regional states such as Iran, Oman, and Bahrain but well before Ab-dulaziz Al Saud (commonly known in the West as Ibn Saud) established what was to become the modern state of Saudi Arabia in 1902.

Qatar's population has climbed from less than 25,000 in 1950 to about 2.6 million in 2020. However, Qatari nationals have remained a small minority; they only number roughly 300,000. The capital and largest city in Qatar is Doha, with a metropolitan area population of more than two million.[1] Qatar is an Islamic state whose laws and customs follow the Islamic tradition, and Arabic is the official language of the country, though English and some South Asian languages are widely spoken.

1.2. Early History

The coastal states of the Arabian Gulf are connected by common civilizational bonds. Archaeological missions have revealed common ties that unite centers of civilization in the Gulf region, from the Stone Age until the Islamic era, on the western coast of the Arabian Gulf.[2] Many civilizational features that combine the modern states of Qatar, Bahrain, and Kuwait have emerged in a group of archaeological sites.[3]

Nearly all of present-day Qatar was submerged under water 100,000 years ago. During the last Ice Age, sea levels receded as the polar ice caps and continental glaciers rose, and the Qatari peninsula emerged. Qatar has a long history, dating back millennia before the spread of Christianity and Islam in the region. As noted,

---

(1) UN Department of Economic and Social Affairs, 2019.
(2) Shaker, 2005.
(3) Al-Duwaish, 2013.

archaeologists have found traces of Stone Age inhabitants dating as far back as 50,000 years ago at coastal campsites and at inland sites where flint could be found and chipped into stone tools. Monuments found on an island west of Qatar revealed the skeletons of inhabitants from before the sixth millennium BCE. Other finds indicate the existence of important commercial maritime activity that dates back more than five thousand years.

Several archaeological studies conducted in Qatar prove that the era of human settlement there dates back to prehistoric times and reveal the importance of the Arabian Gulf in general and Qatar in particular to early civilization.[4] The eastern shores of the Arabian Peninsula are con-sidered the cradle of civilization, from which the Akkadian, Babylonian, and Assyrian civilizations emerged and settled in Mesopotamia (Iraq). At roughly the same time, the Arameans settled in Syria and the Nabateans settled in Palestine and Jordan.

European archaeologists—including a Danish mission in 1965, an English mission in 1973, and a French mission in 1976—unearthed inscriptions, spears, and elaborate pottery, show-ing that the Qatari peninsula has held permanent habitation since the fourth millennium BCE. Traces of pottery have been found in Qatar from the Al Ubaid culture of Mesopotamia. This painted pottery represents the beginning of a continuous archeological record in present-day southern Iraq, predating even the culture of the Sumerians, who invented the first writing system and built the first cities in the world.

As the seas continued to recede, the Qatari peninsula connected to the mainland, and nomadic tribes from the adjacent Nejd and Al-Hasa regions in what is now Saudi Arabia brought their herds to graze. There is also ceramic evidence of connections with the Dil-mun civilization of 4000 to 2000 BCE. Furthermore, stone cylinder seals, both in Mesopotamian and Indus Valley styles, and imported coins dating from 400 BCE have been found in Qatar, indicating a robust trading culture. These artifacts are now on display in the national museums in Doha and Al Khor.

Herodotus, the Greek historian and traveler of the fifth century BCE, reported that Qatar's inhabitants were Canaanites and

---

(4) Scott-Jackson et. al., 2014.

Chapter 1: A Brief History of Qatar

excellent sailors. Alexander the Great's admiral Nearchos sailed Gulf waters, and his logs recorded the skills and secrets of the sailors of Arabia. Nearchos' logs described the geography of the Persian Gulf and mentioned "Catara," making Qatar one of the few Gulf states that has retained its name as it was in its first form since ancient times.[5]

Geographies compiled by the Roman astronomer and geographer Claudius Ptolemy in 150 CE show that Qatar clearly appeared in the peninsula as Catara. The same name also appeared in the Atlas of the History of Islam, where maps identified the peoples of the Arabian Peninsula in the middle of the second century CE and the geographical location of Catara. Ptolemy is credited with devising new methods of cartography in the second century CE, and in his geographic endeavors, he identified more than 6,300 places, including the location of Qatar.

The map of the Portuguese geographer Lázaro Luis, dating back to 1563, is considered one of the most important maps indicating the location of Qatar. The Qatar Peninsula, under the name Catara, is drawn as a clear prominence in the Gulf waters. Qatar was symbolized as a large fortress with four towers and a huge, fortified entrance directly overlooking the Gulf. Some geographical and historical maps in the early eighteenth century CE, including a French map of the coast of the Arabian Peninsula, the sea, and the Gulf, showed Qatar as mentioned under the name Katara.[6]

Greco-Roman trade between Europe and India regularly passed through the Arabian Gulf by 140 CE. Archaeological evidence indicates the presence of both Greek and Roman influence in the Qatari peninsula. Excavations have shown that Qatar was a seasonal fishing station where fishermen went to dry their fish. The two most important commodities that Qatar exported in the Greco-Roman period were pearls and dried fish. In the era of the Persian Sassanian Empire in the third century CE, the Gulf region emerged as the primary commercial center linking the East and the West. The most important goods traded were copper, spices, various types of wood, dyes, textiles, pearls, dates, gold, and silver. Qatar played a prominent role in this trade movement, and it contributed at least two commodities: dyes and precious pearls.

---
(5) Qatar National Library, 2020.
(6) Katara, 2020.

The Sassanians of Persia ruled the Gulf, including Qatar, from the third century CE until the Islamic conquest. In a contemporary encyclopedia of cities, the Arab geographer Yaqut Al Hamwi praised the long cloaks woven in Qatar, called burud qatariyya, that were worn by the Prophet Muhammad and his wife Aisha. The geographer also described spears made in Qatar that he called khattiya.[7]

Qatar was the seat of an important Christian diocese from the third century CE until the Islamic conquest The diocese apparently having jurisdiction over the entire eastern coast of the Arabian Peninsula from Khafji to Hormuz broke away from the Church of Persia around the end of the seventh century.

References in the Syriac Bible, the Peshitta, dating back to the seventh century, describe the prosperity of the "Bayt Qatarya" region. Its people were famous for weaving clothes—"Bayt" in Syriac means house, area, or country. Qatar also produced one of the great fathers of the early Church, St. Isaac (Ishaq) the Syrian—given this name because he wrote extensively in the Syriac language.[8] Today, the Greek Orthodox Church in Doha commemorates his name.

1.3. Qatar in the Islamic Era

The region in which Qatar is located, also called the Bahrain region, accepted Islam peacefully without a fight. Its rulers, Al-Mundhir bin Ayez and Amr bin Abdul Qais, converted to Islam early upon the arrival of the messenger of the Prophet Mohammed to Bahrain, Ala bin Al Hadrami. Islam took root in Qatar with little controversy.

The majority of Qatar's population before Islam were from Bani Amer bin Abdul Qais and then were joined with Banu Saad bin Zaid Manat bin Tamim. The two tribes continued to inhabit Qatar even after the introduction of Islam to the Bahrain region and its spread among the Arab tribes.

At the beginning of the 280s AH (circa 890s CE), a fanatical offshoot of Ismaili Shi'ites called the Qarmatians captured Qatif, Al-Hasa, and Hajar and established their rebel state in Bahrain. Next,

---

(7) Al-Hamwi, approx. 1224.
(8) A detailed history of Qatar's early Christian history and the life of the saint can be found in "The Ascetical Homilies of Saint Isaac the Syrian" published by Holy Transfiguration Monastery (Brookline MA, 2012).

they expanded their influence to include Qatar and parts of Oman. Qatar fell under the rule of the Qarmatians for two centuries, during which the peninsula's economic life rapidly deteriorated due to disrupted roads and high traffic taxes. The Qarmatians also attacked merchants and commercial caravans.

It is worth noting that Qatar had prominent importance in the Middle Ages due to its location as an important stop for commercial caravans that took the land route linking Iraq with Oman and the Arabian Peninsula, perhaps because of its abundance of water and pastures.

After the Caliphate moved from Damascus to Baghdad, Bassorah (present-day Basra in southern Iraq) became the region's main trading center with India and even China. Several Qatari sites participated in this maritime traffic, the most notable being Al Murwab, north of Zubara, which was occupied during the ninth to eleventh centuries CE, and Ruwayda and Al Huwailah, both of which were thriving during the eighteenth century.[9]

Prior to the late eighteenth century, permanent settlements in Qatar were largely based on pearling, fishing, and the presence of a major well. The largest of these settlements, Al Bida, was the forerunner of the modern Doha metropolitan area, now the home to 80 percent of Qatar's population.

1.4. The Europeans Arrive

The Age of Discovery and European expansion to the Americas and the Indian Ocean and Asia brought the first European powers to the Gulf. In 1497, after successfully navigating Africa's Cape of Good Hope, the Portuguese first appeared in the Indian Ocean. In 1507, Portugal launched an expedition to gain control over the trade routes to India and seized Hormuz. The first Portuguese landed in Qatar in 1517. They fought for almost 100 years to gain and hold control of the Indian Ocean's trade. However, they were eventually defeated and reduced to a minor colonial power after numerous wars with Persia and the Ottoman Empire, supported by the Dutch and British who supplanted them.[10] In addition to foreign conquerors, Arab tribes continued to move in and out of Qatar.

---

(9) Al-Marikhi, 1996.
(10) Özbaran, 1972.

For half a century, internal wars wracked the region. The British East India Company's warships suppressed the Gulf sheikhdoms' flotillas and bombarded their ports, ostensibly to stop piracy —and, incidentally, keeping the Gulf Arab trading fleets from the lucrative India trade.

The British did not know the region well at first and tended to lump all the coastal peoples together. For example, unlike the reputation of some Persian Gulf tribes, the people of Qatar do not have a history of piracy. Rather, pearl merchants and fishermen were the mainstays of their economy during the Ottoman period (1871-1916), according to historian Zakaria Qurshun in the Encyclopedia of Qatar. Nonetheless, in retaliation for a maritime raid of unknown origin, a British East India Company ship bombarded Doha in 1821, destroying much of the town and forcing its inhabitants, who did not know why they were being attacked, to flee.[11]

At that time, Qatar was famous for pearl-diving. This industry thrived on the coasts of the Arabian Gulf until the early 1930s.[12] Qatar was distinguished by the abundance and purity of its oyster banks from which many types of pearls were extracted. Historical sources agree that pearls from Qatar were among the finest varieties, and it became famous for producing large, expensive rolled pearls called "Qar."[13]

Pearling was the main craft of Arab coast inhabitants, especially in the summer months, and it played an important role in building the Arab emirates. This is evident from the various taxes imposed by sheikhs on pearl fishermen. Furthermore, some sheikhs operated their own sailboats and owned whatever was collected.[14]

The coast of Ras Abu Aboud, located south of Doha, was one of the most famous ports in Qatar. Residents of the city of Doha would travel to the port on foot, go into the sea, and pick up oysters with their hands. As the weather got warmer, they would dive deeper. In shallow water, they would feel the oysters with their feet. As the water got deeper, they would dive to pick up oysters, take what they collected, and sit on the beach to break them. The

---

(11) Lorimer, 1915.
(12) Katara 2012.
(13) Al-Marikhi, 1996.
(14) Al-Ezzi, 1972.

Tawaweesh (pearl merchants) would visit these individuals on foot to buy any pearls they collected.[15]

1.5. Britain and the Protection Treaty with Qatar

At the same time as the British spread their influence among the coastal areas, more Arab tribes from the Najd were moving to the coasts of Qatar. Among them were the Al Thani, ancestors of the present ruling family. Qatar first appeared as a separate state in 1825, when the Al Thani family united Qatari tribes and completed the "tribe to state" transformation. The Al Thani family settled first in the Sakak area in the south of Qatar, before moving to Ruwais until the independent state was established after signing the protection treaty with Britain.[16]

During the years leading up to the Qatari state's establishment, Britain had become the most powerful actor in the region. After expelling the Portuguese from the Strait of Hormuz in 1622, the British had acquired strong commercial and political influence in the Arabian Gulf. For Britain, Qatar and other Arabian Peninsula sheikdoms became of far greater strategic value in the eighteenth century when the British established control of India and began to monopolize the region's trade with Europe.

By 1798, London had obtained the support of the Imam of Muscat (Oman), the leader who maintained influence among the tribes of the Arabian Gulf, including those of what was to become Qatar. Although Britain had no major rival powers in the region, the British perceived threats to their monopoly of trade with India from local shipping. Once the British suppressed the Arab fleets, the latter often turned to piracy, complicated by wars between local sheiks. Consequently, the British imposed the trucial system via bombardment and several treaties, beginning with the General Treaty of Peace of 1820 and later the 1853 Perpetual Maritime Truce.

The General Treaty of Peace of 1820, between the sheikhs of the Arabian Peninsula's coastal area and the British East India Company, ensured the company's maritime dominance. It also required the sheikhs to recognize British authority and demanded

---
(15) Al-Ghanim, 1994.
(16) Heard-Bey, 2008.

an end to the slave trade (a lucrative business in the Gulf at the time), as well as an end to piracy. The United States did not end its slave trade until 1865, forty years—and a dreadful civil war—later.

Britain signed a separate treaty with Muhammad Al Thani in 1868, setting the course for Qatar's future independence under the consolidated rule of the Al Thani family. The treaty with Britain that recognized Qatar's independence and Sheikh Muhammad Al Thani as the peninsula's ruler established the basis for a monarchical system in Qatar whereby the rights to leadership would be passed down in the Al Thani family. This treaty, in effect, ended the informal style of leadership common to the region, replacing it with a more centralized monarchical system.

This period also marked the establishment of an American consulate in Muscat—the first in the region—in support of New England merchants and their clipper ships.

1.6. Qatar and the Ottoman Empire

During the 1870s, the Ottoman state sought to centralize its authority and strengthen its presence in the Arabian Gulf, challenging British efforts to control the region by granting a limited degree of independence and sovereignty to local sheikhs. The Ottoman governor of Baghdad, Midhat Pasha, occupied parts of Eastern and Central Arabia during the 1870s. At this time, Jassim bin Muhammad Al Thani, considered the founder of the modern state, invited the Ottomans to Qatar.

The Ottomans understood they could not challenge British naval domination in the region; consequently, they attempted to apply pressure on the British from the land. The Ottoman annexation of Qatar and Al-Hasa, strategically located in the center of the Gulf, cut the British off from much of Eastern Arabia. The British perceived this move as a threat to their de facto control of the Trucial States. Consequently, they sought ways to push back.[17]

In 1880 and 1892, the governments of British India and Bahrain signed two agreements that turned the Bahrain archipelago into a British protectorate. In 1888 and 1892, the government and the rulers of the sheikhdoms now part of the modern-day United

---

(17) Althani, 2013.

Chapter 1: A Brief History of Qatar

Arab Emirates (UAE), except Fujairah, signed similar agreements, becoming British protectorates.

The Ottoman presence in Qatar gave the Al Thani emirs a degree of leverage against their foreign interlocutors—both the British and the Al Saud family that dominated the lands to the west.[18] In the following years, however, Qatar's relations with the Ottoman authorities worsened because of the high taxes imposed by the Ottomans. This led to resistance, and in the famous Battle of Wajbah of October 1893, Qataris joined together to defeat the Ottomans.

The Battle of Wajbah positioned Sheikh Jassim as Qatar's uncontested leader, giving him an "aura of authority"—a tribute to his ability to demonstrate that the Qataris were a force and a presence to be respected. The defeat of the Al Khalifah and Abu Dhabi incursion into Qatar in 1867 and the battle of Al Wajbah burnished the small nation's military credentials. Qatar made history by inflicting the first defeat on the Ottomans by local forces. The defeat of the Ottoman garrison at Al Wajbah predated the better-publicized capture of Riyadh by the forces of Abdulaziz bin Saud in 1902 and presaged the final expulsion of the Ottoman Empire from the Gulf.[19] To this day, the State National Day Celebrations Organization Committee recognizes Jassim ibn Muhammad as Qatar's first modern leader to lead the peninsula towards unity.

In the current era, Qataris remember Sheikh Jassim as a ruler who brought security, justice, and prosperity to Qatar. Under his rule, the country witnessed an extensive renaissance and prosperity in all aspects of society and the economy, which was particularly evident in its rise as one of the largest exporters of pearls.[20] The development of improved maritime transport also evolved, and the port, which became ready for the growth of the export, import, and distribution movement, assisted Qatar's economic growth. The number of vessels operating in the fields of trade, diving, and transport doubled, business and sources diversified, the population quickly increased, and Doha rapidly urbanized.

---

(18) Heard-Bey, 2008.
(19) Zahlan, 1979.
(20) Rahman, 2006.

On January 23, 1871, Al-Zawraa, the official Ottoman newspaper of the Baghdad Province, published a report that referred to Al-Bada as the center of Qatar's nascent government. The paper noted that the province contained roughly 1,000 homes and 4,000 people. There were other villages like Al-Wakrah, about three hours' travel from Al-Bada, that by the same estimation contained 200 houses, 400 people, and 50 ships. Al-Khor was mentioned as a village located in the north four hours away from Al-Bada, and it had about 500 houses. Al-Zubarah was mentioned as a third area located near the Bahrain archipelago. In the Ottoman newspaper Taqweem Al-Waqi, 40 villages were mentioned, in addition to the well-known population centers.

Although estimates of the number of places of residence and populations differed in the Ottoman sources, all of the sources agreed that Qatar was one of the most populated areas in the Gulf, with both urbanites and Bedouins. Urbanites lived around water in valleys and cities near oases and worked in fishing, pearling, and maritime trade. The Bedouins, however, roamed the desert and worked by herding camels and sheep or by transporting commercial goods. Bedouin tribes and clans lived communally instead of separately.

A report submitted to the Ottoman Ministry of the Interior indicated that the total population of Qatar numbered approximately 20,000, of whom 8,000 lived in the rif (rural area) and 12,000 in villages. The number of mosques in the rif reached 19, and the same source estimated 15 in the villages. Furthermore, Qatar had 15 primary schools.[21]

1.7. State Formation in Qatar

In 1916, the ruler of Qatar, Sheikh Abdullah bin Jassim Al Thani, son of Jassim bin Muhammad, signed an agreement with Britain that formally put the country under British protection. Although the 1916 treaty brought Qatar into the trucial system, fierce competition from American oil companies seeking concessions in the Gulf forced Britain to seek a closer relationship with the sheikhdoms. In 1935, the British signed a treaty that increased financial payments to Qatar in exchange for the granting of an oil concession to the Anglo-Perian Oil Company.

---
(21) Anscombe, 1997.

Chapter 1: A Brief History of Qatar

The discovery of oil in Qatar in 1939 marked a major turning point for the country. Initially, World War II halted the exploitation of the emirate's oil from 1942 to 1947 and hit Qatar's economy hard (along with the economies of the other Gulf States). It exacerbated economic hardship caused by the collapse of the pearl trade in the midst of the Great Depression. Qatar's economy revived only with the start of oil production in the late 1940s and had the side effect of making the state completely dependent on hydrocarbons. As Michael Field has documented, "almost everyone [in Qatar] who had any significant income at all in the later 1940s drew it from the oil company; for five days of the week, the entire life of Doha seemed to drain away to Dukhan, the oil-company town on the other side of the peninsula."[22]

Oil revenues would significantly contribute to the transformation of the Qatari economy and society, establishing a new basis for Qatar's role in the global arena and its web of foreign relations. Qatar began developing modern government structures and public services in the 1950s, launching the state's first modern budget in 1953. Qatar also witnessed development of its public services during the 1950s, with the first telephone exchange, desalination plant, and power plant opening between 1953 and 1957.

The 1960s saw many other important developments for Qatar. The emirate's infrastructure, foreign labor force, and bureaucracy expanded significantly. Qatar invested in early efforts to achieve greater economic diversification beyond the oil sector, with a focus on cement, fishing, and agriculture, albeit on a small scale.

Until their departure in 1971, the British exercised considerable influence over Qatar's relations with foreign governments. The British were keen to keep states they saw as economic or political threats away from developing relations with the governments of the "protected" states. This antipathy to a foreign presence extended from revolutionary leftist Arab regimes (Nasser's Egypt, for instance) to the United States, which were deemed a threat to British economic interests. For example, the British blocked the United States from opening consulates in the states they "protected" and even restricted the movements of the lone American consular officer allowed to visit Qatar and the Trucial States.[23]

---
(22) Roberts, 2017.
(23) Kennedy, 2002.

Despite Britain's influence, Qatar's internal politics were never immune to global and regional movements and the effects of the Cold War. Arab nationalism and left-wing ideologies began to gain a following in the Middle East and occasionally spilled over into small student demonstrations. However, the small size of the population and the tight family ties kept political dissent from causing serious problems for social cohesion.

1.8. The Development of Qatar's Institutions

When the British announced in 1968 that they would withdraw from "East of Suez" by 1971, the Qataris faced the need to make major decisions in anticipation of the departure of the British—and the British military—from the Gulf. The leaders of Qatar, Bahrain, and the Trucial States contemplated joining a union in the aftermath of Britain's exit in 1971. Because of the political and border differences between the Gulf states, particularly Qatar's dispute with Bahrain on some issues, the union initiative failed and the rest of the Trucial States united among themselves to become the United Arab Emirates.[24]

Thus, the Qatari emir decided that Qatar would have to go its own way and proclaimed a provisional constitution in April 1970. This constitution declared Qatar an independent Arab Islamic state with shari'a law as a foundation for its legal system. One month later, Emir Sheikh Ahmad appointed his cousin Sheikh Khalifa bin Ha-mad Prime Minister, and, on September 1, 1971, Qatar declared its independence from Britain. Qatar Radio broadcast the message that Doha was terminating the "special treaty relations and all agreements, engagements and arrangements arising there from that were concluded with the British Government." Two days later, on September 3, 1971, Britain recognized Qatar's independence. American recognition followed shortly thereafter.

A few months later, Sheikh Khalifa bin Hamad Al Thani assumed the rule of the country on February 22, 1972. His first action was to appoint a Minister of Foreign Affairs and an adviser to the emir, to inaugurate a new phase of government and administrative organization. In June 1995, Sheikh Hamad bin Khalifa Al Thani took the Qatari throne.

---

(24) Zahlan, 19

1.9. Conclusion

Sheikh Hamad's accession to power marked the beginning of a new stage in the contemporary history of Qatar, the launch of a dramatically accelerated process of development and modernization that has changed the lives of Qataris and the status of the State of Qatar beyond recognition. This book will follow those developments at various levels, starting with the economy, passing through the media, and ending with Qatar's support for the rise of less developed countries through investment and charitable development projects. In less than 50 years, Qatar was transformed from a small, impoverished emirate that relied entirely on the pearl trade to one of the richest countries in the world.

Photography

The earliest known depiction of Qatar as "Catara" on Ptolemy's second-century map.

Qatar and the Arabian Peninsula by Jodocus Hon-dius, printed 1598.

Doha waterfront, 1903.

Bedouin tribes in Badia, Qatar's southern rural area, circa late 1940s to early 1950s.

Al-Kuwt, a fort established by the Ottoman Empire in 1880.

Doha, 1950.

Photography

Doha Corniche, circa 1960s.

Members of the Qatari Police in charge of guarding Dukhan Airport during the 1950s.

The Central Post Office building in the late 1960s.

Doha during the 1970s. Note the expanded construction in the background.

The building, runway and parking lots of the old Doha International Airport in 1974.

Doha's International Airport, 1960.

Photography

The palace of Qatar's ruler in Doha, circa 1960s.

Doha docks, 1954.

The Amiri Diwan and clock tower, 1960s.

The Al-Rayyan area outside Doha, 1960.

The Great Mosque of Doha, pictured 1975.

Umm Salal Muhammad Castle, 1956.

Chapter 2
The Early Days of the Qatar-U.S. Relationship

2.1. Introduction

The relationship between the United States and the State of Qatar was formally established in September 1971 when the United States recognized Qatar's independence. The United States recognized Qatar only three days after its declaration of independence, but communication between the two countries had started in the 1930s, most importantly in 1934 when American oil companies first opened commercial ties with Doha.[25] However, the arrival of the first resident American ambassador took another forty years.

Throughout the second half of the 20th century, American interest in Qatar grew. Following the decline of the traditional international powers, the U.S. stepped into the Gulf to ensure the continued flow of hydrocarbons and promote regional security. After the withdrawal of British troops from the region in 1968, U.S. played an increasingly important role in the development and security of Qatar. This relationship has only deepened with time, resulting in the close ties we see today.

2.2. America's Interests in the Gulf Region

In the aftermath of the First World War, the U.S. Geological Survey estimated that American oil supplies would run out in the following decade.[26] This official estimate was a serious concern, as it marked the first time the United States faced a major energy security crisis. At the same time, the British and French had just replaced the Ottomans as the controlling powers in much of the Arab world

---
(25) Qatar Digital Library, 2020.
(26) Council on Foreign Relations, 2017.

Chapter 2: The Early Days of the Qatar-U.S. Relationship

and sought to preserve the region's relatively newly discovered oil reserves for their own interests. This policy rested in large part on the ability of London and Paris to deny access to the region to other powers, including large American oil companies.

In response to British and French attempts to keep American oil firms out of their Middle East protectorates, the United States retaliated by denying access to foreign companies to its areas of control and influence. American oil companies had begun to pursue concessions in Latin America, and the United States tried to obstruct Anglo-French companies there as well. On the other hand, the U.S. government declared an "active oil diplomacy," demanding a reciprocal "open door" policy in the Middle East and insisted on promoting an open political and economic approach by allowing all companies, regardless of nationality, to compete for concessions worldwide.

Although London and Paris refused to completely give in to the American competition, they allowed seven American and other Western companies, acting as a single consortium, to invest in a share of the Iraq Petroleum Company (IPC), which had inherited a de facto monopoly on exploration and production in Mandatory Iraq from the Ottoman-era Turkish Petroleum Company.[27] Five of these seven companies were American: Standard Oil Company of New Jersey, Standard Oil Company of New York (Socony), Standard Oil Company of California (Socal), the Texas Oil Company, and Gulf Oil. The other two major oil companies, Anglo-Persian and Royal Dutch/Shell, remained in British hands.[28]

These companies were among the biggest oil companies in the world; prior to the emergence of state-owned oil companies, they controlled roughly 85 percent of the world's petroleum reserves.[29] In return for their stake in the IPC, the seven companies (known as the "Seven Sisters") committed to not seeking concessions and agreements independent of the IPC in an area spanning Iraq, the Arabian Peninsula, and Turkey.

In 1928, the U.S., French, and British companies, competing for concessions in the region, signed the so-called "Red Line Agreement" that divided up rights to concessions belonging to the old Turkish Petroleum Company (TPC) in Iraq. It also stipulated that the

---
(27) Metz, 1988.
(28) Ibid.
(29) Sampson, 1975.

Chapter 2: The Early Days of the Qatar-U.S. Relationship

participating companies would agree to not develop oil fields within the territory comprising the TPC unless they secured the support of the other members. However, it had a "self-denial clause" that permitted these seven oil companies to dominate production in the region in the following decades. These companies beat the British into Saudi Arabia, signing an exploration agreement with Saudi Arabia's founder and longtime leader, King Abdulaziz bin Saud (ibn Saud).[30]

As would recur repeatedly in the highly volatile petroleum industry, technological advances led to increased oil production then to overproduction and price collapses. Despite the U.S. Geological Survey's dire 1919 estimation, America's oil production more than doubled from 1920 to the 1930s—with the predictable result that oil prices plunged to only a few cents per barrel by 1931. Nevertheless, the big companies soon discovered vast new reserves in the Arabian Peninsula, first in Bahrain and then Saudi Arabia, Kuwait, and Qatar.[31] British attempts to maintain economic monopolies raised fears of political dominance among regional governments under British "protection" such as Iraq and those in the Gulf. They sought to diversify away from British-controlled companies in the 1930s and found ready partners among the Americans. American companies began to strike deals in Iraq independent of the IPC.

In two decades, American oil companies secured access to sizable oil reserves in Iraq and Saudi Arabia, notwithstanding European efforts to block them or scale them down. By 1934, Socal, Gulf Oil, and other U.S. oil companies were holding concessions in the region that served to strengthen Washington's influence. The American oil industry aggressively pursued concessions in many other Arab countries. In addition to the Gulf, American companies soon began to work in Egypt and Yemen. The U.S. government increasingly began to engage in political maneuvering in order to support those American oil companies that were seeking to enlarge their stakes in the region.

In 1931, Washington formally recognized Ibn Saud's government in the Nejd, which fueled more British suspicions about American interests in the region. London correctly understood that American political influence in the Gulf directly supported America's oil industry and harmed British influence. During and after World War II, British

---
(30) Yergin, 1990.
(31) Council on Foreign Relations, 2017.

Chapter 2: The Early Days of the Qatar-U.S. Relationship

suspicions grew significantly over America's ambitions in a region where London's influence had reigned supreme for decades.

During the Second World War, Washington extended its Lend-Lease military assistance program to Saudi Arabia, despite its neutrality until the final days of the war. In 1945, President Franklin Delano Roosevelt met with Saudi King Abdulaziz bin Saud in a dramatic meeting on a U.S. warship in the Suez Canal and established Saudi Arabia as America's principal ally in the Arab world. The meeting also ensured that America, rather than the United Kingdom, would maintain control over Saudi oil.[32]

After the defeat of the Axis powers, Washington continued to give Saudi Arabia development and military aid. The United States also maintained an important air base at Dhahran near the headquarters of the Arabian-American Oil Company (Aramco). In the 1950s, the United States sponsored the Baghdad Pact, a military alliance that sought to bind Iran, Iraq, Pakistan, Turkey, and the UK against Soviet expansion into the region. The Baghdad Pact ceased to function with the 1958 pro-communist Iraqi Revolution, but it remained in effect as the "Central Treaty Organization" (CENTO) until Iran's Islamic Revolution in 1979. This tumultuous period saw the issuance of the Eisenhower Doctrine, an attempt to stop the spread of communism, in 1957, followed by the American intervention in Lebanon in July 1958. In 1962, the United States deployed fighter planes to Saudi Arabia to deter Nasser's Egypt. Almost by accident, Washington was now deeply engaged in the Arab world.[33]

America had set its sights on the region's oil wealth and strategic geography in the 1930s. However, after the Second World War, British power had begun to unravel. Britain's rapid economic decline as a result of the losses suffered in the war, all while America boomed, led to a slow but inexorable displacement of British power in the Gulf and the Middle East.

The British hung on stubbornly, but a series of setbacks, such as the spectacular failure of the Suez Crisis of 1956, made it impossible for the UK to sustain its presence. In 1968, British Prime Minister Harold Wilson's declaration of British withdrawal from "east of Suez" culminated

---
(32) Council on Foreign Relations, 2017.
(33) Riedel, 2019.

in the full withdrawal of British forces from the Gulf in 1971 and the subsequent declaration of independence by the nine Trucial States (later coalesced into the United Arab Emirates), Qatar, and Bahrain.[34]

Over the decades that have passed, Washington's strategic thinking in the hydrocarbon-rich Gulf has focused heavily on sustaining U.S.-friendly governments. However, the volatility of the region has fostered challenges against American power and policy. America's efforts to achieve its economic and national security objectives in the Gulf have been costly, both in terms of money and human lives, but the United States has persevered. The three wars that have erupted in the Gulf since Iran's Islamic Revolution of 1979—the Iran-Iraq War (1980-1988), the Gulf War (1990-1991), and the U.S. invasion and occupation of Iraq (2003-2010)—and the ongoing implications of the 2011 Arab Spring have underscored the region's volatility.

2.3. Roots and Evolution of American-Qatari Relations

American-Qatari relations strengthened with the strategic security partnership between the United States and Qatar in the aftermath of the 1991 Gulf War. This relationship was formalized when Washington and Doha signed the 1992 Defense Cooperation Agreement (DCA).[35] However, bilateral relations date back many decades prior to the Kuwait crisis, even preceding Qatar's independence in 1971. The Americans and Qataris established contacts and links beginning in the 1930s that laid the groundwork for a diplomatic relationship that was formalized shortly after Qatar became an independent country and full-fledged UN member state.

Historical documents in the Library of Congress and the British Archives indicate that the earliest beginnings of the Qatari-American relationship date back to 1935, when an employee of the Anglo-Iranian Oil Company based in Qatar named Charles Clark Mylles wrote reports concerning the activities of certain individuals who came to visit Qatar and meet the sheikhs. Mylles believed that these men were representing the interests of American oil companies and reported that local agents employed by the

---

(34) Pham, 2010.
(35) Katzman, 2019.

Chapter 2: The Early Days of the Qatar-U.S. Relationship

companies were working to have contacts with the Emir of Qatar Abdullah bin Jassim Al Thani (r. 1913-1949) to convince him to grant concessions to U.S. companies.[36]

The American interest in oil exploration gave Qatar significant leverage to enter into serious negotiations with other companies to increase the return from the sale of Qatari crude. A different document, dated January 2, 1934, was sent by the British Political Resident in Bahrain to his superior, the Minister of State for India (at the time the UK administered the Gulf through the India Office). He reported that Abdullah bin Jassim, at the time Qatar's emir, asked for 500,000 rupees per annum in addition to the returns. The Resident noted that "this is an exaggerated demand and that this is inspired by the expectations of the American competition" represented by the Standard Oil Company of California (today known as Chevron).

There is also a volume of 505 pages in the British Library entitled "Private Papers and Records from the India Office, 29 Dec 1933-12 Jul 1935" that is related to the British government's policy towards Qatar in light of the attempts of the Anglo-Persian Oil Company (APOC) to obtain oil concession rights in Qatar. These documents confirm that the British government was keen to have the British company obtain the concession rather than an American oil firm. As a result of continuous efforts and negotiations, the oil concession was granted to APOC in 1935.[37] However, economic deals and oil competition were not the only tools Americans used to get closer to Qatar and its leadership. In 1943, Sheikh Abdullah bin Jassim sought to have a hospital built in Qatar. His son, Hamad bin Abdullah, had an unspecified illness that the sheikh wanted to be treated at home. At this time, residents of Qatar who suffered from serious illnesses needed to go abroad for treatment, mostly to British or American mission hospitals in Bahrain, Kuwait, Iran, or Oman.[38]

In a letter dated December 15, 1946, the British Political Agency in Bahrain discussed how the American Mission in Qatar contributed to helping Qatar financially for a hospital in Doha. Sheikh Abdullah bin Jassim contributed his personal funds to the hospital as well. During

---
(36) Qatar Digital Library, 2020.
(37) UK National Archives, 1972.
(38) Qatar Digital Library, 2020.

Chapter 2: The Early Days of the Qatar-U.S. Relationship

the hospital-building project, the leadership of Qatar sought British assistance in Bahrain, specifically asking for building material. However, the British Political Agency in Bahrain declined, writing that "Bahrain has not got the material to spare." The letter also states that the Political Agency felt "disinclined to help in the establishment of an American assisted dispensary."[39] Britain's decision to not provide Qatar with the funds for the hospital's construction prompted Qatar's leadership to turn to the American Mission for a full partnership to complete the project.

The hospital in Qatar opened toward the end of 1947. The building had beds for 12 in-patients. By the beginning of the following year, roughly 75 outpatients were visiting the hospital on a daily basis. This hospital hired nurses of Indian origin and one Indian doctor named "Dr. George." Additionally, the American Mission sent in one additional doctor at a time on a rotational basis.

One of the prominent doctors first sent to the hospital by the American Mission was Dr. Mary Bruins Allison. She described the hospital in the following way:

"It was an Arab-style house on the seafront. It had a beautiful view but was mostly a walled square, enclosing a large, empty courtyard with two-storied rooms around the edges. We used the downstairs rooms for a clinic and patients and the upstairs rooms for male and female Indian nurses, the cook, and myself. It was not well built. The bathroom was far away and didn't have good facilities. The water was too cold to take a bath."[40]

Dr. Allison was one of the first American women, and the most prominent, to live in the Gulf; she divided her time between Kuwait, Bahrain, Qatar, and Muscat. In her diary, she talks about the stages of development the Gulf countries went through, from traditional to advanced societies that provided their citizens and residents with modern medical services. Mary Ellison and other Western nurses and doctors, especially those associated with the American Mission, provided great humanitarian services, including the introduction of modern medicine in Qatar and the Arabian Gulf through diagnosis, treatment, and surgical operations. After the establishment of this

---
(39) UK National Archives, 1972.
(40) Allison and Shaw, 1994.

Chapter 2: The Early Days of the Qatar-U.S. Relationship

hospital in Qatar, a letter from the British Foreign Office noted how the "excellence of [the American Mission's] medical work has made them popular with the local inhabitants, and it is not surprising that Qatari official (sic) have turned to them for advice and assistance in running his hospital."[41]

Interestingly, the British correspondence makes it clear that in the 1940s the British government was concerned about the growing American influence in the Arabian Gulf as a threat to London's interests. The correspondence referred to the British concern that medical facilities in Qatar should fall into American hands. "There is probably no more effective way of securing influence and friendship amongst the peoples of the Persian Gulf," opined one civil servant, "than by providing them with facilities for the treatment of sickness. The opportunity has however passed for the present, though it may be possible to consider the establishment of… [an] Agency hospital at Qatar at a later stage when our interests there demand a resident Political Officer."[42]

By the late 1940s and early 1950s, the American Mission stopped sending staff members to Qatar to work in this hospital, and the nascent Qatari government began to take complete responsibility for all operations at the facility. However, the Americans continued to be active on both diplomatic and humanitarian levels in Qatar and the Arabian Gulf after World War II, competing with British clout in the region.

Shortly after the Second World War, Washington turned to London for advice and permission regarding the building up of an American diplomatic presence in some of the Arabian Gulf coast states. On March 18, 1948, British officials in London wrote to their colleagues in Bahrain, Kuwait, Qatar, and the other Gulf states to relay that U.S. officials at the American Embassy in London inquired about whether or not the British would be "agreeable" to the establishment of a U.S. consulate in Kuwait to also serve their interests in other Gulf states like Bahrain and Qatar.

---

(41) Qatar Digital Library, 2020.
(42) Ibid.

Chapter 2: The Early Days of the Qatar-U.S. Relationship

A letter dated May 14, 1949, stated that the British diplomats had "no insuperable objection to [the] U.S. proposal" to establish a U.S. consular office in the Gulf region, provided that "there would be no change in question of jurisdiction," the "U.S. Consular Officer would not have direct dealing with [the Kuwaiti] Sheikh," and "there would be no change in political agreements with oil companies which oblige them to deal with the Sheikh through the Political Agent."[43]

Further correspondence between British officials noted that the American government was pressing Britain for an answer about whether or not it would be acceptable for the United States to establish a consulate in the Gulf region. A Foreign Office internal document discussed British ambivalence at balancing interests with the Americans: "We feel that if we refuse them this facility, for which they have extremely strong practical grounds [raises the] danger of that tension mak[ing] some difficulty about [the U.S.] accepting continuance of our position in the Gulf."[44]

In August 1949, a letter from the British Foreign Office outlined London's agreement to permit Washington to open a consulate in Kuwait. Yet the letter stressed that although "we have been most anxious to meet the practical requirements of the United States Government, we have also been seriously concerned at the political repercussions which are likely to arise."[45] Across the Atlantic Ocean, American diplomats also recognized how the United States and Britain had conflicting interests in relation to Qatar and other parts of the Arabian Gulf. A State Department document from 1947 defined their differences:

"Kuwait, Qatar, the Trucial Coast, Muscat, and Oman are so primitive that any industrial development in these areas, other than the development of oil, will have to wait for some time. It was long the British policy to keep the people flanking the sea route to India in a state of primitive economy. The United States has rather the opposite point of view, however, and is anxious to develop the agriculture, industry, and trade of an area like the Arabian Peninsula. This is based on the theory that the more developed an area becomes the more it can produce, the more it

---
(43) Qatar Digital Library, 2020.
(44) Ibid.
(45) Ibid.

Chapter 2: The Early Days of the Qatar-U.S. Relationship

will buy from the United States and other countries of the world, thereby increasing the sum total of world trade, and prosperity. This American policy of pushing the economic development of the Arabian Peninsula may run counter to British thinking. It should be possible, however, to show the British that our policy is to their interest in the long run."[46]

The same document continued outlining American attempts to push the British into allowing greater American penetration in the region, including Qatar:

"The sparsely habited promontory of Qatar, the six petty Sheikhdoms which make up the Trucial Coast, and Oman & Muscat are under concession to Petroleum Development Company Ltd., a subsidiary of Iraq Petroleum, in which Socony Vacuum and Standard of New Jersey each have 11.75% interests. Development work has at last been started in Qatar, and it would be desirable to induce Petroleum Development Company, Ltd., either to start work in their other areas or else to relinquish its concession."[47]

This report from the U.S. State Department listed various non-oil interests that the United Kingdom had in the Gulf, including aviation, banking, construction, insurance, shipping, and mining; it also noted:

"As the historic conditions which favored British financial, commercial and other developments in the area change, the influence of those interests as anchors [for the British] may be considerably altered... In connection with the Persian Gulf States of Kuwait, Qatar, the Trucial Coast, Oman and the Hadhramaut [southern Yemen], British influence has been largely a 'dead hand.' The world demand for oil, plus American representation in the oil companies involved, is beginning to bring about activity in Kuwait and Qatar. We hope that competition from American capital and enterprise will stir the British into greater economic activity in these outlying areas."[48]

---

(46) U.S. State Department, 1947.
(47) Ibid.
(48) Ibid.

Chapter 2: The Early Days of the Qatar-U.S. Relationship

Noted also was the British tendency to keep Yemeni trade bottled up behind Aden: "This situation should be corrected, pehaps by the development of a Yemeni port on the Red Sea."[49]

During Dwight D. Eisenhower's presidency (1953-1961), various issues in the Middle East fueled friction in London-Washington relations—most notably the Suez Crisis of 1956 that pitted Britain, France, and Israel against the unlikely diplomatic alliance of the Unit-ed States, the Soviet Union, and Egypt. However, a territorial dispute at Al Buraimi was also a source of friction between Saudi Arabia, in America's sphere of influence, and Oman and the Trucial States, under British suzerainty. The dispute led to an armed clash between the Trucial Oman Scouts and the Saudi White Army, two forces that had respectively been trained by British and American officers.

Yemen was another issue of contention between the two western powers. A White House Memorandum of Conversation dated January 30, 1956, explained how the "Saudi Arab question" and the Al Buraimi territorial dispute "brought forth the greatest difference between the British and Americans." Washington had "good relations with Saudi Arabia" and was dependent upon oil reserves from the Arabian Gulf. In the conversation, British Foreign Secretary Selwyn Lloyd, according to the memorandum, stressed London's view that British "prestige in the whole Middle East and its status in the Arab Sheikhdoms, including Kuwait, depended on its ability to support the Sheikhdoms." He also emphasized that "any indication of weakness on its part would place the British position in jeopardy."[50]

Six and a half months later, U.S. Secretary of State John Foster Dulles wrote a letter to his British counterpart expressing his interest in learning about London's "plan to raise formally the possibility of Saudi Arabian access to the sea near Qatar." Dulles stated that the U.S. government was "certain that there are other possible territorial adjustments, too, which could be explored." In light of the Suez Crisis, Dulles said that American leadership continued to believe "that the preservation of our joint position in the Arabian Peninsula and the Gulf can be more satisfactorily insured by reaching accord." As Dulles

---
(49) U.S. State Department, 1947.
(50) Ibid.

argued: "if a definite treaty boundary between Saudi Arabia, Kuwait, Qatar and the Arab principalities could be found which the United States and the United Kingdom could support publicly and firmly for the future, we would have gone far toward removing a problem which otherwise seems destined to plague us for a long time."[51]

2.4. America Exploits Britain's Departure

After Harold Wilson announced the British withdrawal "east of Suez" in 1968, the United States began preparing for new realities in Qatar and other Arabian Gulf states. The British formally withdrew in 1971, and Qatar and other sheikdoms of the Gulf coast gained their independence.

The Americans were keenly concerned about this new development. A National Security Council staff memorandum dated December 31, 1969, stated that "UK withdrawal is now a fact of life in the area. Gulf States have already started adjusting to UK absence, and this process is irreversible."[52] U.S. diplomats at the time identified several challenges for Washington to address in light of this new reality. These included the Shah of Iran's ambitions in the Arabian Gulf, the Arab states' hostile reaction, issues over the division of maritime borders in the Gulf, and the Kremlin's growing attention to the region.

The complete withdrawal of British military forces in 1971 raised the question of whether the United States should replace Britain as the dominant security provider in the region. But the decision in Washington was firm in rejecting such a possibility. The United States at that time was completely involved with its military intervention in the Vietnam War. Moreover, both the U.S. Congress and the American public had become increasingly disappointed with U.S. military intervention abroad. Therefore, international and domestic considerations prompted U.S. policymakers to exclude the possibility of new security commitments in the Gulf region.

The NSC memorandum outlined what it saw as key American interests in the sub-region that needed to be secured at the time of the British exit. These included military interests, flight privileges across Iran, Gulf coast states, Qatar, Kuwait, and Saudi Arabia, and

---

(51) U.S. State Department, 1988.
(52) U.S. Department of State, 1969.

promoting "stability" in order to mitigate the threat of Soviet gains and the rise of "radical" Arab regimes/movements. At the same time, Washington was keen to factor into account the fact that roughly 15,000 U.S. citizens lived in the Gulf, whose oil was "crucial to West Europe, Japan, and U.S. forces in [Southeast] Asia."

The document stated that the United States was in no position to replace the British presence, so it was in Washington's interests to "urge greater cooperation among Gulf states themselves, especially Saudi Arabia and Iran." The National Security Council staff cautioned against "giving [the] impression of 'backing out,' or else we weaken our friends, undermine stability, and encourage USSR." Concerning Soviet aims in the Arabian Gulf, the document observed the history of Russian ambitions in the body of water, dating back to the Czarist days, maintained that the Soviets sought to "supplant Western presence," and pointed to the USSR's naval visits to the Gulf.[53]

The memorandum assessed that encouraging the British to maintain their presence to help counter Soviet expansionism in the Arabian Gulf was "unacceptable in London and unworkable in the Gulf." Furthermore, the United States embracing a "do nothing" policy in the Arabian Gulf would constitute an "abdication of responsibility from which our interests would surely suffer" considering the "tremendous importance of the area to us."

Additionally, the document highlighted the sensitivity of the Palestinian issue vis-à-vis Qatar, Kuwait, Saudi Arabia, and other Arabian Gulf sheikhdoms:

"Many Palestinians live in the Gulf States. Shaykhs raise money for fedayeen. 'Palestine question' is an irritant in our relations with moderate Gulf Arabs; if that conflict remains unsettled, the outlook is for 'steady erosion' of the U.S. position in the Gulf. Arab-Israeli tension also affects Arab-Iranian relations, since Iran has ties with Israel."[54]

---

(53) U.S. Department of State, 1969.
(54) Ibid.

Chapter 2: The Early Days of the Qatar-U.S. Relationship

2.5. Qatar Formalizes Relations with Washington

Qatar began preparing for its independence in 1968 when London announced its intent to withdraw. The leadership in Doha was forced to make sensitive decisions that needed to be finalized prior to the British exit. Sheikhs Ahmad Bin Ali and Khalifah Bin Hamad proclaimed a provisional constitution in April 1970. This constitution established Qatar as a newly independent Arab state with full sovereignty over its internal affairs and foreign policy. In May 1970, the ruler of Qatar appointed Sheikh Khalifah Bin Hamad to serve as the country's prime minister.[55]

On September 1, 1971, Qatar declared its full independence from the United Kingdom; two days later, Britain affirmed it, and on September 3, Qatar finally secured its official independence. The official relationship between the United States and Qatar was established on March 19, 1972, when U.S. Ambassador William A. Stoltzfus, Jr. presented his credentials to Qatar's ruler. But Stoltzfus remained in Kuwait, not Qatar, and he was the sole American diplomat representing Washington to the newly independent countries in the Arabian Gulf during the initial period of time that followed the British departure.

The newly independent Gulf States found this arrangement unacceptable, and the State Department scrambled for resources to open Embassies in three newly-minted capitals: Doha, Manama, and Abu Dhabi. Finally, the US established its embassy in Doha on February 24, 1973. About one year later, on August 22, 1974, the first resident US Ambassador to Doha, Robert P. Paganelli, presented credentials.

On February 22, 1972, the Qatari throne was transferred to Sheikh Khalifah Bin Hamad in a "soft coup" that the United States saw as beneficial. On June 28, 1972, the State Department sent Secretary William P. Rogers a telegram that stated, "Qatar is better off under new Ruler who is most sensible man in Gulf."[56]

Most historians have pinned the beginning of US-Qatar relations to this period between 1971 and 1973. Indeed, this was the time in which formalized bilateral relations between Washington and Doha were established. Yet the formation of contacts, engagement, and coordination between the Americans and Qatar, as this chapter illustrates, preceded Qatar's independence by several decades.

---

(55) Chan, 2016.
(56) U.S. Department of State, 1972.

2.5. Conclusion

The early years of the Qatar-U.S. relationship are defined by narrow national interests and the relative power of actors within the Gulf. The actions of individual Qataris and Americans notwithstanding, contacts between Qatar and the U.S. were minimal compared to the deep relationship the two countries enjoy today. During the colonial period, the U.S. played a hands-off role in Qatar, focusing on hydrocarbon exploitation. However, geopolitical events in the latter half of the 20th century drove Washington to pursue an increasingly close relationship with Qatar. In time, the bilateral engagement fostered in 1971 have come to shape the outlook of both countries and have transformed U.S. engagement with the Gulf region.

Photography

> POLITICAL AGENCY
> BAHRAIN.
>
> D.O. No.C/1384.   The 15th of December, 1946.
>
> My dear Pelly,
>
> Will you please refer to your demi-official letter No.3139 of the 30th September, 1946?
>
> 2.   The position as regards the "hospital" at Dohah is that a few years ago the Shaikh of Qatar started to build a "hospital". The funds for this were provided in part, I believe, by the American Mission and possibly the Shaikh gave some money himself. I believe also that the Mission provided some money for drugs. I am pretty sure that my information is correct, but I hesitate to ask the Mission.
>
> 3.   The Shaikh of Qatar has now written to me asking for assistance in importing building material for the dispensary from Bahrain. Bahrain has not got the material to spare at the moment, and so the building is likely to remain in the unfinished state it has been in for the past few years. Furthermore I feel disinclined to help in the establishment of an American assisted dispensary.
>
> 4.   There is, however, need for medical facilities at Dohah and I should like to be in a position to assist the Shaikh in the provision of drugs, equipment, building material and also a doctor. Now that Petroleum Concessions Limited's activities are growing this would appear to be the proper time to increase His Majesty's Government's prestige and this would follow the establishment of a dispensary. I suggest we should follow the precedent of the Trucial Coast.
>
> The budget figures for the Trucial Coast are:-
>
> | | | Rs. |
> |---|---|---|
> | 1. Pay of Establishment | | 4,600-0-0 |
> | 2. Allowances (Dearness Allowance, Travelling Allowance, etc.) | | |
> | T.A. 1,000 | | |
> | D.A. 2,000 | | 3,000-0-0 |
> | *3. Hospital Contingency & Medical equipment | | 1,600-0-0 |
> | | | 9,200-0-0 |
>
> *(Utilised for purchasing medicines, bandages, and other miscellaneous equipment for the hospital)
>
> Pay of Establishment is as under:-
>
>   (Cont'd)
>
> C.J. Pelly, Esq., O.B.E., I.C.S.,
>   Secretary to the
>   Hon'ble the Political Resident
>   in the Persian Gulf, Bahrain.

British report on American attempts to secure an oil concession in Qatar, 1934-1935.

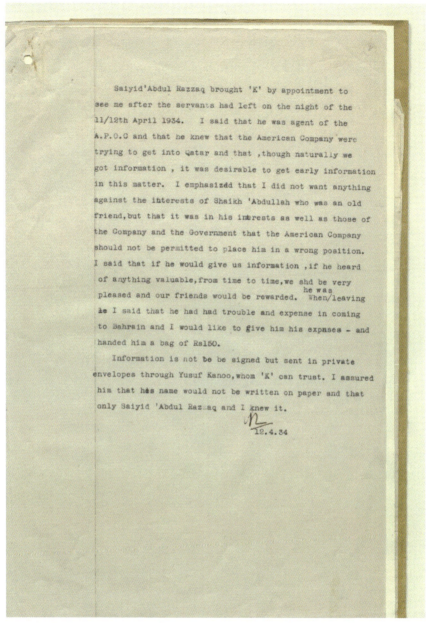

British report regarding construction of American Mission Hospital in Doha, 1946.

Photography

American Chevrolet in Qatar, circa 1930.

American made cars at Doha airport, 1930s.

First Qatari hospital under construction in partnership with American Mission, 1945.

Qataris receiving treatment in the hospital.

Women and children in the hospital.

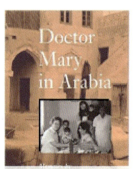
Autobiography of Dr. Mary Bruins Allison

Chapter 3
From Pearl Diving to the Global Economy

3.1. Introduction

When the British established their protectorate over Qatar in 1915, it was a poor country whose economy depended almost entirely on fishing and pearls. As Blake Hounshell wrote, "For most of its short history, Qatar has been an afterthought of an afterthought in global politics, an impoverished backwater that had often fallen prey to the schemes of stronger powers."[57] As disc sed later in this chapter, Qatar rose from poverty to become a middle-income country after the development of its oil resources in the latter half of the twentieth century. It did not reach its current status as the richest per capita country in the world until the development of its liquefied natural gas capacity at the beginning of the twenty-first century.[58]

---

(57) Hounshell, 2012.
(58) Ibid.

Chapter 3: From Pearl Diving to the Global Economy

3.2. The Pearl-Dependent Economy

Before the discovery of oil in western Qatar in 1939, the peninsula had a maritime economy that relied heavily on the pearl diving industry. As Sheikh Muhammad Al Thani explained to the British traveler William Palgrave during his visit in 1863, "we are all in Qatar and the Gulf from the highest to the lowest we all work in pearl-diving."[59]

To keep up with the European and North American demand for pearls that reached a peak toward the end of the nineteenth century, Qataris worked hard in the pearl industry. Qatari men went out on pearl diving missions that typically lasted three to six months at a time. With the launch of the pearl seasons, pearling boats would carry approximately 20 men. When it was impossible to travel because of disasters, natural crises, or the lack of financial resources necessary to prepare for the trip, men would go to work in simple farming and herding because of the desert climate. British historical documents and records indicate that no other pearl center in the world had a higher proportion of its population engaged in the industry than Qatar.[60]

The difficulties and hardships of working in this dangerous industry made Qataris proud of their history as pearl divers in past eras. The diving profession was one of the most difficult in the region, and there were many stories about the extent of suffering a pearl diver risked.

The occupation's challenges were represented in the lengthy trip, difficult goals, weak tools, and other problems, especially the unpredictability of nature, the madness of the sea, and the hazards of diving. The lack of oxygen and fast changes in water pressures coupled with sharks, snakes, barracudas, and other marine predators in the Arabian Gulf compounded the dangers of this line of work.

Outcomes would sometimes be harsh. Pearl divers often lost their lives or suffered life-long serious injuries and illnesses. One researcher wrote:

---
(59) Qatar Tourism Authority, 2019.
(60) Ibid.

Chapter 3: From Pearl Diving to the Global Economy

"*Without modern technology, pearl diving was extremely dangerous. The men didn't use oxygen tanks; instead, they pinched their noses with pieces of wood and held their breaths for up to two minutes. They would also often wear a sheath made of leather on their hands and feet to protect them from the rocky surfaces found below. The divers would throw a rope with a rock tied at the end into the water and then jump in. These divers would often descend over 100 feet below, quickly use their knife or a rock to pry oysters and other mollusks from rocks on the seafloor and place the oysters in a rope bag that they had hung around their necks. When they could hold their breath no more, the diver would pull on the rope and be pulled back up to the boat.*"[61]

Notwithstanding the perils of diving for pearls, its profits motivated Qataris to continue to work in this industry despite the suffering and pain. Pearl diving also shaped the nature of social relation-ships in Qatar. For example, rulers, who played a significant role in the profession, had little else as a course of revenue except for taxing pearl boats. As one scholar explained, "In 1907 the boats of Doha and Wakra paid four Maria Theresa silver dollars annual[ly] for each captain, diver, and hauler. The shaikh of Wakr(ah) collected MT $3,400 annually, the shaikh of Doha MT$8,400."[62]

In Qatar and elsewhere in the Arabian Gulf, pearl-dominated economies established hierarchies "within a segment labor force broken up into merchant-moneylenders, ship captains (nakhodas), and the divers and haulers who undertook the dangerous task of collecting the pearls from the seabed," wrote Middle East scholar Kristian Coates Ulrichsen. "It also spawned a derivative service economy that supported and sustained it."[63]

Unfortunately, Qatar's geography and the peninsula's distance from overland trade corridors kept it from developing as an institutionalized trade hub. Consequently, although Qatar had some merchants before the discovery of oil in 1939, it lacked a true merchant class.[64]

---

(61) Qatar Tourism Authority, 2019.
(62) Crystal, 1990.
(63) Ulrichsen, 2015.
(64) Fromherz, 2012.

Chapter 3: From Pearl Diving to the Global Economy

The pearl diving industry, which had given Qatar a measure of wealth for centuries, abruptly collapsed in the first half of the twentieth century. In the mid-1920s, Japan created cultured oyster farms that ultimately glutted the global market with cultured pearls. A few years later, the Great Depression of 1929 caused a major decline in North American and European demand for pearls and other luxury items.

The collapse of the industry led to a dark time in Qatar. As Ulrichsen put it, the pearl industry's decline in the country was "a disaster which almost overnight removed the one export on which the people of the Gulf could rely to bring in foreign earnings." Although the decline of the pearl industry caused economic pain all over the Arabian Gulf, its effect was arguably most harmful in Qatar, which had virtually no lucrative economic activity outside of the pearl diving sector. The other three pearl-producing countries—Bahrain, the Trucial States, and Kuwait—were also affected but had established themselves as major Arabian Gulf ports, lessening the effects some-what.[65]

Although Qatar ceased to be a pearl-diving country almost eight decades ago, the pearl remains a symbol of the country's heritage and culture, as it does for other Arabian Gulf states. Qatar continues to employ the pearl in traditional stories and has made it prominent in museums, paintings, drawings, urban projects, banknotes, and public monuments. Qataris continue to celebrate this aspect of their culture and heritage with annual pearl diving competitions.[66]

Moreover, a series of annual celebrations and competitions centered on the pearl are held at the Cultural Village of Katara to revive this culture and remind the new generation of Qataris of their history and the heritage of their ancestors.

3.3. Discovery of Oil and the Boom Era

When oil was discovered in southwestern Persia in 1908—and 19 years later near Iraq's Kirkuk—the Middle East changed forever. Due to the eastern Arabian Peninsula's geological conditions being similar to those of Iran and Iraq, exploration commenced in the Gulf coast states and other Arab countries soon after the initial discoveries of oil.

---

(65) Ulrichsen, 2016.
(66) Ibid.

Chapter 3: From Pearl Diving to the Global Economy

In 1932, the Bahrain Petroleum Company (BAPCO) discovered oil in Bahrain. In 1938, Standard Oil of California struck oil in Saudi Arabia along the Eastern Province's Arabian Gulf coastline, and oil was discovered in Kuwait that same year.[67]

Britain and the United States began to compete for oil in the Persian Gulf in the early 1920s, raising the stakes in regional territorial disputes and demonstrating the need to demarcate territorial borders. In 1922, American negotiators made an effort to include Qatar in an oil concession that they were negotiating with Saudi King Abdulaziz Ibn Saud. The British, Qatar's "protectors," were quicker and more active in the negotiations and blocked the American approach to Qatari territories.[68]

The first oil survey of Qatar in 1926 by the Anglo-Persian Oil Company (APOC) found no indication of oil in that specific area, but after more exploration, other areas were discovered. After an oil strike in Bahrain, interest increased in Qatar for more exploration. When geological surveys suggested the presence of oil, negotiations began to give way to agreements. Britain succeeded in signing an agreement with Qatar's ruler Sheikh Abdullah Bin Jassim through Anglo-Persian representatives after lengthy negotiations.

The signed 75 year concession agreement began on May 17, 1935. The agreement provided for Qatar to receive 400,000 rupees (roughly $150,000) on the initial signature and then 150,000 rupees (roughly $65,000) per annum once production of oil began. The British also made other specific promises of assistance.[69] To abide by the terms of the Red Line Agreement negotiated between the United States and Britain, Anglo-Persian transferred the concession to the Iraq Petroleum Company (IPC) subsidiary company Petroleum Development (Qatar) Ltd.[70]

IPC struck oil one year after it began to drill its first well in Dukhan, on Qatar's west coast, in October 1938. However, the demands of World War II paused development and export between 1942 and 1947, worsening the financial difficulties that Qatar and the other Gulf states faced.

---

(67) Metz, 1994.
(68) Wilkinson, 1991.
(69) Qatar Digital Library, 2020
(70) Office of the Historian.

3.4. Early Economic Development

Modern economic development in Qatar began after the discovery of oil reserves when, in late 1937 and early 1938, three geologists, Norval E. Baker, T.F. Williamson, and R. Pomeyrol, paid a visit to the Qatari peninsula's western coast to locate a drilling site in Dukhan. In the 1940s, shortly after the discovery of the country's hydrocarbon re-sources, Qatar signed agreements with America-based Superior Oil and Central Mining and Investment before ultimately signing a deal with Royal Dutch Shell in 1952.

Although oil was discovered in Dukhan in 1939, Qatar did not begin commercially producing oil until 1949, as World War II prevented additional exploration.[71] Despite this, as Qatar's economic transformation into the oil period began, such changes had a profound impact. In the words of Jill Crystal, "oil had an immediate and radical effect on the base as well as the peak of Qatar's social structure." Qatar's major pre-oil industry, pearl diving, was already under decline from foreign pressure; it quickly became irrelevant from an economic standpoint. By 1955, virtually all non-oil economic activity was limited to "some small overland trade with Saudi Arabia."[72]

The oil transformation fundamentally changed social structures in Qatar. Qataris previously employed in the pearling industry in Qatari villages, as well as Qatari nomads, received jobs in the oil sector. These would form a "working class" that eventually transformed into a economically productive, active social class, giving birth to a new Qatari identity during the oil era.

The oil phase brought about a pivotal qualitative leap in Qatari society through resources for development and building institutions and facilities. As Qataris continued to benefit from oil wealth in the 1960s, with the discoveries of major oil fields toward the end of the decade, there were notable booms in the areas of education, health, and other services. The number of schools, students, teachers, hospitals, and healthcare professionals all increased drastically during the two decades that followed the discovery of oil in the peninsula.[73]

---

(71) Sorkhabi, 2010.
(72) Crystal, 1990.
(73) Nasser, 2014.

Chapter 3: From Pearl Diving to the Global Economy

Qatar's internal economic transformation had major ramifications internationally. By 1960, Arabian Gulf States were producing about 15 percent of the global supply or oil, a number that doubled by 1970. The West's post-war economies became highly dependent on oil from the Middle East, chiefly the Gulf region. In 1950, for example, the United Kingdom sourced 81 percent of its oil from the Middle East, illustrating the extent to which Qatar and other Gulf oil exporters became of paramount economic and geopolitical value to Western powers in the post-war period. In 1961, one year after the establishment of the Organization of Petroleum Exporting Countries (OPEC), Qatar joined the cartel.[74]

Important to Qatar's economy was the discovery of the country's largest oil reserve, Bul Hanine, in 1972, shortly after Qatar gained its independence. From 1973 to 1982, a renewed oil boom brought significant wealth to Qatar. Production levels peaked at approximately 500,000 barrels a day. At the same time, in stages between 1973 and 1977, the Qataris nationalized their oil economy from the British, with the establishment of Qatar General Petroleum Company (later renamed Qatar Petroleum) in 1974.

The dramatic increase in prices that followed the 1973 Yom Kippur War and the 1979 Iranian Revolution sent revenues skyrocketing. As a result of oil's overnight surge, Qatar underwent rapid industrialization, and its administrative state grew concurrently. Due to the oil boom, the Qatari government became a net distributor, rather than an extractor, of wealth to its citizens, and this pattern has continued to the present day.[75] The windfall in oil revenues enabled Qatar, like the other Arabian Peninsula states, to establish a well-funded welfare state for its citizens.

In 1981, oil prices peaked before beginning a decline due to decreasing international demand and a market glut from overproduction. The consequences of falling oil prices during the 1980s severely harmed the Qatari economy (as well as those of the other Gulf States). In 1986, oil prices collapsed, plummeting to historic lows below $10 a barrel. By 1985, Qatar had run its first budget deficit since before the oil era, which persisted through

---
(74) Conway, 2015.
(75) Ulrichsen, 2016.

the 1990s. During this era, GDP per capita fell from $31,100 in 1984 to $15,070 in 1994.

3.5. Natural Gas Creates the World's Richest Country

Despite the importance of oil to Qatar's modern transformation in the second half of the twentieth century, it was ultimately natural gas that enabled the small nation to become the wealthiest country per capita in the world.

In 1994, Qatari leadership took a risky but ultimately farsighted decision to invest in the still-unproven technology of liquefied natural gas (LNG), seeking to exploit their country's possession of the world's largest non-associated natural gas field, Qatar's North Dome. In what proved to be another farsighted decision, Qatar signed an agreement with Iran in 1969, demarcating the thalweg (median line), the first Gulf country to do so.[76] That agreement demarcated the maritime border between the two countries and gave Qatar control over somewhat more than half of the gas field. By 2009, the North Dome Field constituted approximately 14 percent of the world's proven natural gas reserves.

Qatar's natural gas extraction was not an easy road but a long and hard one. Initially, the Qataris and the international oil companies that had discovered the North Dome Field in 1971 delayed the decision to exploit it until two decades later. Given its distance from the biggest markets, the then-available technology for transporting gas raised doubts about the profitability of investment.

The Iran-Iraq War (1980-1988) further inhibited a Qatari decision to develop the North Field, in part because of its contiguity to Iran's South Pars field. According to Ulrichsen, "investors and consumers (especially Japan) were nervous about becoming overly reliant on natural gas from such a regional flash-point."[77]

The end of the Iran-Iraq War opened the door for Doha to resume negotiations with Tehran. The two governments reached a further agreement in 1989 on how to divide the development of the field. The development of Qatar's LNG industry faced a setback in

---

(76) Diba, 2014.
(77) Ulrichsen, 2016.

1992 when British Petroleum unexpectedly broke its joint venture with Qatargas and withdrew from its concession in the North Dome Field. However, Mobil Oil and the government of Qatar finally made the decision to complete the project in the early 1990s. The results and outcomes bore fruit in the early 2000s when LNG shipments began to the Far East.

The Qatari leadership in agreement with its American partners decided to build the port of Ras Laffan as a major LNG hub prior to signing an agreement with Japan, its first international customer. The initial agreement with Japan provided for annual LNG shipments of 4 million tons.[78]

Qatar's decision to make major investments in the country's natural gas infrastructure sector, nearly two decades after the discovery of the North Field, has strengthened Qatar's international importance. By concluding long-term LNG contracts with these countries and their governments, Qatar created an attractive investment opportunity and preceded other countries that had invested in the same sector. The long-term vision of Emir Sheikh Hamad bin Khalifa also enabled Qataris to benefit from the country's gas wealth, making Qatar a dynamic force in the Middle East despite its small size and population.

Qatar's rise was not only driven by oil and gas but also by the wise leadership of the country. The world before the 1990s did not view LNG as a viable technology. The initiative, direction, and decisions of the Qatari leadership in investing in the LNG sector and exporting it to the world have dramatically increased the importance of Qatar—making it the market maker in the LNG sector, roughly the same as Saudi Arabia in the crude oil sector.

If the discovery of oil in the peninsula in 1939 was considered a great blessing for Qatari society, the outputs of the natural gas sector enabled the state to achieve unprecedented prosperity without relying on the country's limited oil capacity. Today, natural gas output dominates the Qatari economy and plays the same role as did pearl diving in the past.

---

(78) Kanady, 2018.

Chapter 3: From Pearl Diving to the Global Economy

3.6. The Modern U.S.-Qatar Economic Relationship

As one of Qatar's largest foreign investors, the United States has developed important, long-lasting trade relationships with Qatar that continue to grow.

The United States is the largest foreign investor in Qatar's oil and gas sector. According to official statistics, over $5 billion in bilateral trade was concluded between the United States and Qatar in 2015. U.S. exports to Qatar include aircraft, vehicles, electrical machinery and equipment, optical and medical instruments, and pharmaceutical products. America's imports from Qatar include fertilizer, aluminum, and liquefied natural gas. The United States-Qatar Open Skies Agreement has been in effect since 2001, and air travel between the two countries has increased nearly tenfold over the past decade. Qatari commercial relations with the United States have created thousands of American jobs.[79] Today, there are more than 650 American companies in the Qatari market, 120 of which are fully owned by American citizens.

Qatar and the United States share a commitment to developing human capital and work to create flexible, knowledge-based economies with an emphasis on education, openness, and opportunity for all. Economic legislation and reforms recently implemented by Qatar are expected to enhance the investment environment, attracting more American investors, and the volume of bilateral trade has increased in recent years.[80]

Qatar and the United States have also signed a number of economic cooperation agreements. These include an Economic, Commercial and Technical Cooperation Agreement, an Air Services Agreement, and other agreements on matters such as civil aviation security. Most importantly, the two countries have signed an agreement to protect mutual investments, a memorandum of understanding between the Qatar Chamber of Commerce and the Arab American Chamber, and a memorandum of understanding in the areas of energy science and renewable and alternative technical cooperation.[81]

---

(79) U.S. Census Bureau, 2020.
(80) U.S. Trade Representative, 2020.
(81) Ibid.

Chapter 3: From Pearl Diving to the Global Economy

In September 2015, the Qatar Investment Authority opened its first office in the United States to ensure better communication with its current and future American partners. The Qatar Investment Authority aimed to increase and enhance investments in the United States, especially in 2017 when Emir Sheikh Tamim announced the intention to make huge investments in the American market during the following five years, which would result in thousands of new American jobs.[82]

The Qatar Investment Authority allocated $45 billion for investments covering the period between 2015 and 2020, of which $10 billion was directed towards investment in the infrastructure sector. These investments constitute about 23 percent of the GDP of the State of Qatar. Additionally, Qatar's private sector investments in the United States, including Qatar Petroleum, pumped more than $15 billion into the gas, technology, hospitality, and real estate sectors, a significant contribution to the American economy.

In one notable deal, the Qatar Investment Authority and the American real estate investment fund Douglas Emmett announced the acquisition of a $365 million housing complex in California. This project enhances the diversity of the Qatari-American joint investment portfolio, which aims to build a strong partnership in three major sectors: energy, real estate, and infrastructure. It also increased Qatari investment in the United States while reducing the focus on investment in Europe and other countries.[83]

The jewel in the crown of Qatari investment in the United States was in the reconstruction and development of CityCenterDC, a multi-use project in the nation's capital. This was the first and the most important Qatari investment in the U.S. real estate market. Qatar's investments in the United States are diversified and include the fields of technology, media, entertainment, energy, real estate, and many others.[84] Qatar also participates with American firms in major development projects in the United States. The Golden Pass LNG terminal in Texas, a partnership between ExxonMobil and Qatar Petroleum, is the most important of these.

---

(82) Knecht, 2019.
(83) Reuters Staff, 2019.
(84) Finklestein, 2011.

Chapter 3: From Pearl Diving to the Global Economy

Qatar Petroleum and American companies have other extensive investment partnerships for international exploration, including a partnership with ExxonMobil in a significant natural gas discovery located in Cyprus. Qatar Petroleum has also formed an alliance with ExxonMobil that won exploration rights off the coast of Argentina.[85] In continuation of their successful partnership, Qatar Petroleum and ExxonMobil announced that they would invest in a $10 billion project to expand the existing LNG import terminal (Golden Pass) in Sabine, Texas, and convert the terminal to export U.S. natural gas.

In June 2019, Qatar Petroleum and the American Chevron Phillips Chemical Company signed an agreement to develop an international petrochemical complex on the coast of the Gulf of Mexico. This agreement, the second of its kind, strengthens Qatar International Petroleum's portfolio in the United States and is one of the company's major growth centers. The agreement also strengthens Qatar Petroleum's partnership with Chevron Phillips, expanding Doha's ties to American oil firms.

The project, named American Gulf Coast Chemicals 2, is expected to be launched in 2024. It will include one of the largest ethane crackers in the world, with an annual production capacity of two million tons of ethylene, in addition to two high-density polyethylene production units. Qatar Petroleum will own a 49 percent stake in the $8 billion project, while Chevron Phillips, through its 51 percent stake, will oversee and manage the project. The two companies also announced their intention to build a petrochemical plant north of Doha in Ras Laffan Industrial City; it will be operational by 2025 and include the largest ethane cracker in the Middle East.

Qatar Airways has also concluded contracts to purchase 332 U.S.-made aircraft, worth about $92 billion, over the next 25 years. These purchases have created more than 527,000 jobs. In July 2019, Qatar Airways entered into an additional agreement with American air manufacturer Boeing to confirm an order to purchase five Boeing 777 freighters in a ceremony at the White House. The agreement, worth $1.8 billion in total, was signed by Akbar Al-Baker, CEO of

---

(85) Reuters Staff, 2019.

Chapter 3: From Pearl Diving to the Global Economy

Qatar Airways Group, and Kevin McAllister, CEO of Boeing, in the presence of the Emir of Qatar and President Trump.[86]

With the continued investment partnership between Qatar Airways and its U.S. counterpart, Qatar Airways' cargo operations have grown significantly over the past years. With the three Airbus 300-600 aircraft purchased in 2003, Qatar Airways currently operates globally scheduled flights on 23 cargo aircraft, in addition to dispatching cargo on more than 250 passenger aircraft.

In October 2015, in order to continue to enhance dialogue and understanding and strengthen relations between the two partners, Qatar and the United States launched the first Qatari-American economic and investment dialogue, representing a major breakthrough in bilateral economic relations. The dialogue serves as an annual forum to bring together decision-makers to enhance financial, investment, and economic ties. These meetings have recently expanded to include forums for strategic dialogue between the two countries. Qatari trade missions to the United States bring together hundreds of businesspeople and investors. The dialogues between the two sides focus on specific sectors such as defense, trade, the investment environment in Qatar, sports, and the World Cup 2022 events.[87]

The first meeting of the Qatari-American strategic dialogue in January 2018 provided a framework for subsequent encounters. Qatar organized a major trade mission to the United States, with the participation of about 120 businesspeople and representatives of 21 Qatari government agencies at all levels. The mission visited a number of American cities to provide American companies an opportunity to learn more about business opportunities and mutual cooperation in Qatar.[88]

Additionally, the United States assisted the State of Qatar in accomplishing its food security strategy, as laid out in Qatar Vision 2030. This partnership was of particular importance during the Gulf Crisis when Qatar was blockaded by its neighbors from June 2017 until January 2021.

---
(86) Constantine, 2019.
(87) U.S. Department of State, 2015
(88) Cronk, 2018.

Chapter 3: From Pearl Diving to the Global Economy

The United States played a major role in helping Qatar overcome the effects of the Gulf crisis. Numerous U.S. cabinet officers, including American Secretaries of State, Defense, and Commerce, visited Qatar after the blockade began. During his 2019 visit, Secretary of Commerce Wilbur Ross emphasized that the trade relationship between the United States and Qatar had created more than 20,000 jobs in the United States, and that America had helped Qatar to achieve the goals of its National Vision 2030 and host the 2022 FIFA World Cup. The Secretary added that the significant investment recently announced by Qatar in the United States would further enhance the two nations' broad and growing economic partnership.[89]

To strengthen American commercial investment in Qatar, the American Chamber of Commerce was launched in Doha in February 2010, becoming the first foreign Chamber of Commerce established in the country. The Chamber works to enhance the growing activities and services of its members in Qatar and America and aims to expand the circle of commercial relations between the two countries. Robert Hagar, President of the American Chamber of Commerce in Qatar, described the group's mission:

"The chamber aims to build strong working relationships between Qatar and the United States. These relationships are not limited to American companies operating in the State of Qatar, but also include all companies that have a desire in real business in the United States. The chamber is expanding its portfolio of activities to serve companies, decision-makers and individuals wishing to join its active community, and is looking forward to receiving more members in response to the growing interest of American companies to expand their activities by working in the State of Qatar."[90]

---

(89) Ross, 2020.
(90) U.S.-Qatar Business Council, 2020.

3.7. Conclusion

The development of the deep and profitable economic and commercial ties between the United States and Qatar followed as a logical development from the fantastic growth of Qatar from one of the poorest countries in the world to the richest. The discovery of oil in the 1930s certainly contributed to Qatar's meteoric development. However, the role of U.S. companies—who provided key capital and technical support to the emirate well before it became a state—cannot be overlooked. Today, this interplay between the U.S. and Qatari economies persists. This relationship underpins cooperation in many fields of importance to both countries, such as education, security, health, and sports.

Photography

Sheikh Abdullah bin Jassim visiting a Qatari oil field, 1947.

The first well- Dukhan 1- was drilled in the 1940s.

Construction began on the Doha Port, seen here, in the early 1950s.

An oil tanker control tower in Umm Said in the 1950s.

Beginning of construction of the Doha port in 1950s.

Early gas station for the Qatar Petroleum Company, circa mid-1960s.

Photography

An export terminal for Qatar's liquid natural gas (LNG), seen today.

Hamad Port in Doha.

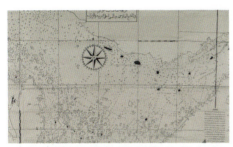
A pearl map of the Gulf, used by Qatari divers.

Qatari pearl divers, mid-1930s.

Qataris celebrate traditional dhows, historically used for pearl diving and fishing.

A traditional Qatari fishing boat.

Chapter 4
Domestic Governance: From Traditional to Modern

4.1. Introduction

Qatar's progress from one of the most traditional societies in the Middle East to perhaps the most progressive rests upon a rich tradition of social equality that once prevailed across the region's tribal and Bedouin societies.

Qatar holds a place of pride as the first nation in the Gulf region to truly address human rights issues. No objective observer contests the assertion that Qatar now has the best human rights standing in the region. Unlike its neighbors, Qatar does not hold political prisoners and does not torture, kill, or otherwise abuse dissidents. Moreover, to a much greater extent than any other country in the region, women have reached a high level of economic and social equality.

Following international criticism of its labor practices, Qatar initiated wide-ranging reforms that have made its labor conditions among the best in the Gulf. The nation enjoys near-total freedom of the press, freedom of speech, and academic freedom. Though much still needs to be done, the country's sweeping accomplishments over less than 30 years are points of pride for the young nation.

Building on its traditions, Qatar developed its National Vision 2030 as a forward-looking framework for advancing human rights in the process of its social and economic development. Its drafters attached significant importance to contributing to international peace through development and humanitarian assistance, and this is an integral component of Vision 2030.

Qatar built its accomplishments on a foundation of reasonable tolerance that has always characterized the people of the country. This tolerance created fertile ground for the extension of participatory government, political freedoms, women's rights, and religious freedom.

4.2. A Century of Evolution in Governance

Qatar's evolution towards participatory government—what Westerners would describe as "democracy"—rests on a solid foundation of traditional tribal governance by consultation and consensus. It has long antecedents in the Arabian Peninsula, predating Islam by millennia.

The advent of oil dramatically changed the power relationship between the ruler and the rest of Qatari society. Before the oil boom, the ruler depended on the small tax revenue generated by customs and the annual levies on the tribes—who did not always want to pay if they saw no value. The relationship between ruler and ruled changed when, in the absence of local law on the extraction of subsoil wealth, British law applied and the oil belonged exclusively to the government, i.e., to the ruler. Because he no longer needed to collect taxes from his subjects, he no longer needed to consult them, laying the seeds for autocracy.[91]

Public services in Qatar developed slowly. Telephone exchanges, desalination plants, and power plants were constructed in the mid-1950s. The government also built a port with a dock and customs warehouse, a small airfield, and a police headquarters.

When world oil prices tanked at the end of the 1950s, the emir had to contend with demands for better wages among oil field workers compounded by unhappiness within the ruling family. In the early 1970s, the revenues of Qatar improved with the recovery of oil prices after the 1973 Yom Kippur War and the Iranian Revolution in 1979. Indirectly, these two events contributed greatly to the acceleration of progress and growth that Qatar achieved during the 1970s and early 1980s. The Qatari leadership succeeded in using oil revenues to create a modern welfare state, thus becoming a "distributor of wealth to its citizens rather than an extractor of it."[92] At the time,

---

(91) Morton, 2017.
(92) Fromherz, 2012.

Chapter 4: Domestic Governance: From Traditional to Modern

Qatar managed to achieve such a high level of continuous spending because it had an indigenous population of less than 50,000 and an unprecedented amount of oil wealth.[93]

In the 1980s, oil prices and revenues decreased again, leading to an annual deficit in the Qatari government's budget that continued into the 1990s. These deficits affected public policy and national development during the reign of Emir Sheikh Khalifa bin Hamad Al Thani and his heir, Sheikh Hamad bin Khalifa. In an attempt to diversify, the two emirs spurred the development of Qatar's vast reserves of natural gas.[94] Consequently, in the late 1990s, a new era began with the growth of the country's natural gas sector, especially liquefied natural gas (LNG). The first liquefied natural gas was produced in Qatar in January 1997, representing a quantum leap in Qatar's LNG revenues and financing more transformations in the Qatari economy.[95]

4.3. Qatar's Unique Political Environment

On the surface, Qatar is not different from other Gulf States: it is a hereditary emirate ruled by a ruling family. However, during the first decades of its rule, the political leadership established a close relationship between the state and Qatari society at large. Although the emir appoints the prime minister (who has always been a member of the ruling family) as well as the Qatari cabinet members, the government is mostly composed of technocrats rather than members of the royal family.[96]

From the perspective of other member states of the GCC, the voluntary transfer of power in Qatar to the younger generation was upsetting. Qatar's pursuit of political and economic reform, and regional and international alliances, following the Gulf crisis in 2017, have also made the other Gulf States worry about the precedent of a Gulf state following an independent political trajectory.

After Sheikh Hamad ceded power to Emir Tamim, the new ruler quickly made his mark on governance in Qatar by making the first of several government reshuffles in June 2013. These appointments enabled a younger generation of policymakers to take

---
(93) Library of Congress, 2020.
(94) Ulrichsen, 2016.
(95) Hashimoto et. al., 2004.
(96) Sergie, 2018.

Chapter 4: Domestic Governance: From Traditional to Modern

over, causing major changes in the implementation of Qatar's national strategy by preserving and diversifying economic gains through the completion of large development projects at home and strengthening the investment sector abroad.[97] The introduction of new ministers and technocrats to higher positions was matched at lower levels by enhancing technical expertise within government ministries and state-related companies.

During the past three decades, the transformation in Qatar has been vast. The requirements of modern state institutions and sectors have grown significantly—particularly since, after the influx of foreign workers, the population of Qatar has increased from about 500,000 in 1995 to more than 2.8 million by 2019.[98] Also, it became apparent that every aspect of state governance should be reconfigured—including the executive and regulatory authorities, the legislative and judiciary process, the development of infrastructure, and the completion of "mega-projects."

The Shura Council (Majlis), established in 1972, is the most powerful legislative body in Qatar. It currently has 45 members, all appointed by the emir and drawn from the professional sectors in the Qatari community. While the Council lacks full consultative authority, it can deliberate on many issues such as the annual budget, propose new legislation, and make recommendations on general issues of state policy. The Council may also request to question ministers if necessary. In November 2017, four women were appointed to the Shura Council for the first time; one of these women, Dr. Hessa Sultan Al-Jaber, became the first woman in the history of Qatar to be appointed to both the Shura Council and the Council of Ministers.[99]

Furthermore, the decision to create an elected municipal council was first broached officially by the emir in 1996 and then discussed in great detail by the Shura Council for two years before the emir approved a final version. The Shura Council made significant modifications to the proposed legislation; for example, rather than launching several municipal councils for Doha and a series of smaller

---

(97) Casey-Baker et. al., 2014.
(98) World Bank, 2020.
(99) Al Jazeera, 2017.

Chapter 4: Domestic Governance: From Traditional to Modern

councils across the country, the Council successfully persuaded the emir to create a single, larger council for all of Qatar within Doha (home to 80 percent of Qatar's population).

Defining suffrage for the election took up a large part of the Majlis' deliberations. A lively debate ensued on establishing eligibility based on age, gender, and educational levels. Numerous iterations went to the ruler who returned them to the Majlis, demanding a firm recommendation. Finally, the Majlis agreed that Qatar's very first elections would enfranchise every Qatari over the age of 18, regardless of race, religion, political affiliation, or, crucially, sex.[100]

Due to this decision, Qatar became one of the few countries in the world whose very first elections gave women and men equal rights to vote and stand for office.[101] Elections to the Central Municipal Council were first held in August 1999. Female candidates have run in all the semi-annual elections and have won seats every term except 1999.[102]

After the first Municipal Council elections, the then-emir, Sheikh Hamad, announced the need for a modern, permanent constitution and established a committee to draft it. The emir defined what he believed the proposed constitution should deal with in a historic speech delivered on the occasion. Sheikh Hamad set out the basic outlines of the anticipated constitution: it would organize the powers and system of government, determine public rights and duties, and lay out the fundamental guiding principles of state policy while maintaining the importance of Islam and Arab traditional values. The emir concluded that the constitution would seek to enshrine a "popular participation in governance while recognizing the Arab and Islamic traditions of the populace." 32 Qatari scholars and academics made up the constitutional committee. After two years of deliberation, the committee presented a draft to the emir on July 2, 2002, and a referendum to approve was held on April 29, 2003. The referendum had no significant political opposition and passed by an overwhelming margin.

---

(100) Co-author's personal interviews and experience.
(101) Commins, 2012.
(102) MENAFN, 2019.

Chapter 4: Domestic Governance: From Traditional to Modern

The constitution provides for an Advisory Council with significant legislative powers of 30 elected members and 15 appointed by the emir. Despite the delay in scheduling elections, the Constitution remains the law of the land with all of its guarantees while adhering to the traditions of the country. The constitution states that the emir, for example, must consult with the "Ruling Family and the notables in the Country" before designating a Crown Prince.

The constitution also provides for an independent judiciary. The Qatari civil court system has a well-defined structure that exists independently of the emir and his ministers. The Minister of Justice of Qatar may supervise the function of the courts, but he may not otherwise interfere in their judicial function.

The Qatari government has also established and strengthened institutional guarantees to monitor and improve the quality of decision-making and governance in the country. Among these reforms is the Administrative Control and Transparency Authority (ACTA), which was created by Emiri Decree No. 75 in 2011. The agency was reorganized and strengthened by a subsequent decree issued by Sheikh Tamim in 2015. The ACTA worked to implement the charter of public officials' integrity and strengthen awareness of and commitment to public service ethics. In 2016, the Qatari leadership launched the Sheikh Tamim Award for Excellence in Combating Corruption as the first international award of its kind awarded each year on International Anti-Corruption Day. The prize is awarded by the Rule of Law and Anti-Corruption Center (ROLACC), an entity established by the new Qatari leadership in 2013.[103]

These initiatives and actions show a greater focus by the Qatari leadership on building the capacities of community institutions in public and private life at a domestic level. At the regional and international level, Qatari initiatives have supported various international institutions, NGOs, and civil society organizations that have contributed to the public sphere, policy-making structures, and the decision-making scene in Qatar and at the Gulf, Arab, and international levels.

---

(103) The Peninsula, 2019.

4.4. Freedom of Expression

Qatar was the first Arab country to formally eliminate its Ministry of Information and, as a consequence, abolish censorship. As noted earlier, state organizations do not exercise prior censorship on electronic and print journalism. In fact, freedom of the press is supported by many relevant laws and regulations. Article 48 of Qatar's Constitution states that: "Freedom of the press, printing and publishing is guaranteed in accordance with the law." The Qatari Press and Publications Law of 1979 affirmed the right to work in the press and the duties and obligations of the journalist in accordance with the provisions of the constitution.[104]

Qatari legislation provides a higher degree of protection against libel than most Western democracies. However, this inhibits the press less than societal norms. Much as in other conservative societies with small populations, the local print and electronic press tends to avoid controversy that might embarrass people or stringently criticize the government.

Qatar has also striven to be known as a beacon for academic freedom. Its invitation to the nine foreign universities of Education City came with the promise that they would enjoy complete academic freedom, including in the subjects taught, the selection of faculty, the composition of classes (to include both genders), and the independent selection of textbooks. While controversies sometimes occur—in one 2014 incident a textbook was banned without warning or consultation—the universities continue to operate more or less as their American counterparts would.

4.5. Women's Rights

Qatari women have gained as much or more in legal and societal status as any other country in the region. Since Sheikh Hamid bin Khalifa took power as emir and began the modernization of Qatar in the mid-1990s, his wife, Sheikha Mozah bint Nasr Al-Misnad, took the lead in developing institutions that enabled the women of Qatar to advance further than those of any other Gulf country.

The unique status of women in Qatar is reflected in the country's heritage. Qatar was a commercial society based on pearl diving, a trade that requires long voyages and significant time spent

---

(104) Al-Meezan, 2020.

Chapter 4: Domestic Governance: From Traditional to Modern

away from the home. As a consequence, while their husbands and sons were absent on pearl-fishing voyages, Qatari women normally ran family affairs in their absence.

In the modern era, Qatari women have continued the outspoken pursuit of their rights. The first modern school in Qatar opened in 1951. When it refused to accept female pupils, a woman named Amana Mahmoud opened a school for girls in her own house. It soon received recognition and became the Banat Al-Doha (Doha Girls) Elementary School. When Qatar University opened its doors in 1973, its entering class consisted of 103 women and 54 men.[105]

Qatari women continue to represent more than two-thirds of college students—and an even greater proportion of college graduates—in the country. Although precise numbers are difficult to gather, in the last few years, the number of women traveling abroad for graduate study has anecdotally equaled or surpassed the number of male graduate students.[106]

Qatar was the first Arab country in the Gulf to allow women the right to vote and run for public office. The first Qatari elections were deliberately scheduled for March 8, 1999, to coincide with International Women's Day.

Many prominent women have served, and continue to serve, in prominent positions in Qatari society. Dr. Hessa al-Jaber (George Washington University, PhD) served as Minister of Information and Communications Technology from 2013 to 2016. Prior to that appointment, Dr. Hessa served as the first Secretary General of the Supreme Council of Information and Communication Technology (ictQATAR), an organization devoted to taking Qatar into the IT world of the twenty-first century which later morphed into the Ministry of the same name. During her tenure as Secretary General, Dr. Hessa oversaw the liberalization of Qatar's telecommunications market, ushering in an era of choice and competition.

---

(105) Kubaisi, 1979.
(106) Statistics on Qatari students abroad are decentralized and not easily available.
(107) Durham, 1984.

Another woman, Dr. Sheikha al-Misnad, the first Qatari woman with a foreign PhD, served as President of Qatar University from 2003 to 2015 and played a leading role in the modernization of Qatar's educational system.[107] Dr. Sheikha has published more than 50 articles in journals at home and abroad.

Other prominent female academics include Dr. Sheikha Ahmed Al Mahmoud, who became Minister of Education in 2003. In 2010, Sheikha Maha Mansour Salman Jasim Al Thani, a law school graduate from Qatar University, became the first female judge in Qatar. The appointment of a woman, Lolwa Al Khater, as the first official spokesperson for the Qatari Ministry of Foreign Affairs, marks another milestone.

But it is not the stars that illustrate the importance to Qatar of its women. Labor force participation for women in Qatar is roughly 58 percent—a higher percentage than the average noted by the UN, in the United States, and, indeed, in every other Arab country.[108] Unlike Qatar's neighbors, any qualified Qatari woman seeking work can find it without legal restriction. This has, of course, produced the normal headaches of any modern labor force, but Qatar has addressed these issues as well as any country in the Western world. Child care has never been a significant obstacle to women's employment in Qatar because many grandmothers are still at home and the country's wealth allows for the employment of household staff in large numbers.

4.6. Religious Tolerance

Sunni Muslims constitute an overwhelming majority of the native population of Qatar, and Sunni Islam is enshrined in the constitution as the country's official religion. For several decades after the creation of the modern state, followers of other religions, including Christianity, had to practice their faith in secret. In the 1990s, amid other social and economic reforms, the situation changed dramatically as Qatar turned towards openness, tolerance, and acceptance, allowing followers of Christianity and other non-Islamic religions to practice their rituals and worship free from interference.

---

(108) World Bank, 2019.

Chapter 4: Domestic Governance: From Traditional to Modern

In 1996, Qatar welcomed a priest from the Greek Orthodox Patriarchate of Jerusalem who provided Easter services for the country's European and Arab Orthodox communities in Doha. The relationship developed, and in 1999, the emir of Qatar welcomed the Greek Orthodox Patriarch of Jerusalem, Diodoros II, on an official visit.

Shortly thereafter, the government announced that it was prepared to allow Christian churches to be established in the country. The government provided a large area in Doha's southern suburbs for the construction of churches and built the entire necessary infrastructure. Since then, Qatar has liberalized significantly and has granted greater tolerance of Christianity and other non-Muslim creeds. Perhaps not coincidentally, the Orthodox priest who came to Qatar in 1996 assumed the title of Patriarch Theofilos III of Jerusalem nine years later.[109]

Beginning in 2003, several Christian denominations began constructing churches in the government-provided church compound. A Roman Catholic Church opened in 2005, soon followed by an Anglican church. These were the first Christian churches built in Qatar since the arrival of Islam in the seventh century. The government built the entire necessary infrastructure and provides normal municipal services at no cost to the 19 churches now operating there. As described by Al Araby, the churches currently "stand as a lively symbol of the growing non-intrusive Christian expatriate population in Qatar, a Muslim-majority country influenced by the Wahabi thought, a conservative movement within Islam's Sunni branch."[110]

As Qatar opened to more foreign workers, the number of Christians in the country increased steadily, from approximately 3,900 in 1970, to about 70,000 in 2005, to more than 210,000 in 2015, and 350,000 in 2019. Although the Qatari government does not gather data on religion, anecdotally, roughly 13.8 percent of the resident Qatari population identifies as Christian, an increase of 250 percent over a period of 45 years.

---

(109) Yeanos, 2019.
(110) Castelier and Poure, 2018.
(111) CIA World Factbook, 202

Almost all of the Christians in Qatar are foreigners, and the majority of them are from the Philippines, India, and the Arab world. Other members of the Christian community in Qatar belong to Western and African societies. Catholicism is the largest Christian sect, and other sects practicing in Qatar include Copts, Anglicans, Greek Orthodox, and Syriac Orthodox, almost all of which have American members.[111]

4.7. Labor Rights

Until the last few years, Qatar, much like every other country in the Arab world, had a mixed record on the treatment and management of foreign workers. In the GCC countries, the situation was aggravated by the fact that foreign workers greatly outnumbered the citizen population. In Qatar, this proportion exceeds 90 percent of the workforce.

For decades, most of the world overlooked abuses such as the kafala (guarantor) system, which prevented foreign workers from changing employers or leaving the country without their employer's permission. Kafala laws have been a feature of national law throughout the Arab world for generations.

The kafala system arose from the requirement in national law that the employer "guaranteed" all the debts and infractions of law committed by his foreign employee. For this reason, the employer was given near-total control over employees' activities. However, the restrictions originally conceived to protect the employer later became an instrument of abuse toward the employee. In addition, unscrupulous recruiters in the country of origin, combined with equally unscrupulous employers in the GCC countries, would contract new workers at a stated wage, loan them the money for transportation, and then charge fees based on the contracted wage rates —all treated as a loan with high interest rates.

The employee would arrive in the GCC country to discover that their prospective employer would not honor the wage rates specified in the contract. Because the new worker would still owe inflated amounts to the recruiters, and usually had their passport confiscated on arrival, they would have little choice but to take the job. International human rights organizations had criticized all the GCC states, including Qatar, for these abuses for many years, but comparatively little had been done until events of the 2010s shined a spotlight on the region.

Chapter 4: Domestic Governance: From Traditional to Modern

With the outbreak of the 2017 Gulf crisis, international human rights organizations found an easy target in Qatar, already under a massive public relations assault from its neighbors. Preparations for the 2022 FIFA World Cup had created a huge increase in the foreign workforce and a great deal of publicity over the award of the world's biggest sporting event to such a small country. While all GCC states were complicit in the abuses of the kafala system, Qatar's relative openness to the foreign press and foreign observers made it easier for these groups to criticize Qatar.

Qatar initially responded defensively to the accusations of labor exploitation. However, Qatar's leaders quickly realized that fixing the issues in question would do more to preserve the country's reputation and international ties than ignoring them and stonewalling their critics would. For this reason, over the last five years, Qatar has become a regional leader in improving wage payment systems, strengthening workplace safety and occupational health inspection systems, improving workforce recruitment procedures, enhancing legal protections for workers, and prosecuting violators of workers' rights.

The nation has established a ground-breaking Wages Protection System, unique in the region that addresses the entire chain of labor abuse from recruitment to working in Qatar. Under the new system, recruiters must give potential workers a contract signed by their future employer detailing the wage rate. This contract must then be approved by the Ministry of Labor before a Qatari consulate will issue a visa. On the worker's arrival in Qatar, the employer must establish a bank account in the worker's name at a Qatari bank and arrange to deposit the wages owed according to the contract. The Central Bank monitors the accounts and will notify the Labor Ministry if an employer fails to deposit the wages. Crucially, if they fail to deposit the wages, the Ministry will penalize the employer and take the wages in arrears from the employer's account.[112] The state has even established a fund for the support of foreign workers who find themselves in trouble.[113]

Qatar officially abolished the kafala system in late 2019. The only other GCC state to effectively end kafala, the UAE, did so in

---

(112) International Labour Organization, 2019.
(113) Amnesty International, 2018.

late 2020. In late 2019, the International Labor Organization (ILO) recognized Qatar's efforts to advance social justice and promote decent work conditions. The ILO praised Qatar's enactment of legislative and executive measures in the period from 2018 to 2019 to enhance the rights of migrant workers and noted in particular the country's abolition of the kafala system.[114]

4.8. Advancing Human Rights

Qatar has placed special emphasis on the development of legislation, based on international standards, for the promotion and protection of human rights. It has acceded to seven of the most fundamental international agreements in this field, including the International Covenant on Economic, Social and Cultural Rights; the International Covenant on Civil and Political Rights; and the Law Regulating Political Asylum.

Qatar has continued to develop legislation to support and enhance the role of women in all areas. Article 34 of the Qatari Constitution enshrines the full political participation of women and guarantees equality between all citizens in rights and duties. The Department of Family Affairs at the Ministry of Administrative Development, Labor and Social Affairs was also established to perpetuate the principle of the need for a supreme national government body that deals with the family, and in particular women, in line with the Qatar National Vision 2030.

The Emiri Decree-Law No. 38 of 2002 established the National Human Rights Commission to promote and protect human rights and public freedoms and to consolidate human rights principles and culture. The National Human Rights Commission was reorganized by Decree Law No. 17 of 2010, granting it full independence and an independent budget. Since its establishment, the Commission has implemented programs and activities in Qatar in cooperation with government ministries, institutions, and departments, as well as with domestic, regional, and international civil society organizations. The Commission also works with the specialized human rights organizations and agencies of the United Nations and human rights institutions in many countries.

---

(114) International Labour Organization, 2019.

In January 2020, Qatar announced that it would teach human rights in schools starting in 2021, a move considered the first of its kind in the Gulf region. This was done during the inauguration of the National Human Rights Commission in Qatar, on the sidelines of Qatar's International Book Fair. The Ministry of Education announced an educational curriculum that would include "evidence of human rights education for the preparatory, elementary and secondary levels" (as a reference and a guide to curricula). The curriculum included several subjects, among them the right to identity, play and leisure, education and health, dignity, equality, origin and development, freedom of opinion and expression, privacy, and justice.[115]

4.9. International Human Rights Cooperation

Qatar has developed an institutional framework for cooperation with other countries and United Nations human rights mechanisms to guarantee the protection and promotion of human rights. In one example of this international cooperation, Qatar hosts the United Nations Center for Training and Documentation in the Field of Human Rights for Southwest Asia and the Arab Region. The Center, in its first year of operation, has achieved much through targeting the needs of unemployed youth in the region, the demographic most vulnerable to exploitation by extremists. In addition to skills training, the Center works to educate youth about freedom of opinion and expression to combat hate speech and discrimination.[116]

In 2018, Qatar joined the two most important international covenants on human rights, the International Covenant on Civil and Political Rights and the International Covenant on Economic, Social, and Cultural Rights. In 2019, Qatar promulgated the Law Regulating Political Asylum, the first country to do so in the GCC.[117]

Working to facilitate civil society organizations, the Qatar Foundation for Social Work was established in 2013 as a higher institution that supervises institutions and centers concerned with social work in the state, including (1) The Center for Protection and Social Rehabilitation, (2) The Consultation Center Family, (3) Orphan

---

(115) Middle East Monitor, 2020
(116) NHRC, 2009.
(117) Human Rights Watch, 2018.

Care Center, (4) Empowerment and Care Center for the Elderly, (5) Al Shafallah Center for Persons with Disabilities, and (6) Social Development Center.

4.10. Conclusion

The Middle East, and the Gulf region on particular, is not known for its democratic development. As several scholars have noted, there is a correlation between mineral wealth and a lack of political freedom. In a country without natural resources, a ruler has greater accountability to the people because he must rely on them for financial support. This is seen in the early American demand for "no taxation without representation" that preceded its independence from Britain.

In the Gulf States, this model is turned on its head. Wealthy GCC states such as Qatar, Saudi Arabia, Kuwait, and the United Arab Emirates do not require taxes from their people—a reason that income taxes are either nonexistent or very low in each of the Gulf states. Because the governments of these countries are net distributors, rather than takers of wealth, they do not cultivate popular support to function. For this reason, Qatar could theoretically forego a constitution, ignore human rights, and maintain absolute power within the ruling family. Instead, Qatar's concessions have set it apart from other countries in the Gulf and, indeed, many other countries around the world. In Qatar, advancing the welfare of the people— even non-Qataris, such as the hundreds of thousands of laborers working on construction projects for the 2022 World Cup— has served as the government's primary objective. In doing so, Qatar has proved that it is not simply a traditional monarchy, but a thoroughly modern state—politically and socially, as well as economically.

For the past 30 years, Qatar has sought to set the regional trend for labor rights, women's rights, and political pluralism. The nation has reaped the political benefits of these trends—international human right watchdogs such as Human Rights Watch and Amnesty International have given it credit for its improvements, although much work remains to be done.

Photography

The Amiri Diwan, 1923, originally served as a residence and office for the ruler.

Qatari Shura Council session, 1980s.

Current Amiri Diwan, interior.

Sheikh Khalifa addressing the Qatari Shura Council, 1972.

The Amiri Diwan today.

Qatari Shura Council, 2020.

Photography

Council of Ministers General Secretariat in Qatar.

A church in Doha.

The headquarters of the Qatar National Human Rights Committee (NHRC).

Qatar's first female minister, Sheikha Al Mahmoud, appointed in 2003.

Qatari votes in the first Shura Council Elections, 2021.

Two winning female candidates in the 2019 municipal elections.

Chapter 5
A Small State with a Global Influence

5.1. Introduction

On rare occasions in history, small states acquire outside influence in regional and world affairs. In ancient times, a few Greek city-states gained power beyond their size, albeit briefly. In medieval Europe, Venice's establishment as the financial capital of Europe helped it to acquire near-world power status. Today's Qatar, despite its small population, plays a similar role in its partnership and cooperation with the international community, through a fortunate combination of great wealth, ambitious leadership, employment of active soft power, and a close relationship with the United States.

Unlike many other states that "punch above their weight," Qatar eschews military power. Instead, it has wielded a careful mixture of diplomacy, mediation, and humanitarian assistance. By providing value to powerful allies, especially the United States, Qatar has managed to gain far greater strategic clout than its small size might indicate.

5.2. The Expansion of American Security Interests

Qatar's military alliance with the United States has its roots in the Gulf War of 1991. Qatar sent a small but effective force to join in the fight to liberate Kuwait from Saddam Hussein's Iraq. In a notable historical incident during the Battle of Khafji, a small Qatari regiment stopped a large Iraqi armored division that had just punched through the coalition lines near the Saudi border. The fierce confrontation continued for two days until the city of Khafji was liberated by the international coalition forces.[118] Since then, the relationship has evolved into one of deep strategic cooperation.

---
(118) Middle East Monitor, 2020

Chapter 5: A Small State with a Global Influence

In 1992, Qatar and the United States signed their first formal defense agreement. This agreement formalized the status of U.S. military members in the country, regularized the use of Doha International Airport by the U.S. Air Force, and provided for the construction of the U.S. Army's largest forward prepositioning base in the world near the Doha suburb of As-Sayliyah. The U.S.-Qatar relationship deepened further after 2003 when U.S. forces moved from Saudi Arabia to Qatar and established Al Udeid Air Base, which soon became the key hub for American military operations in the Middle East.

The Qatari-American military relationship has been successful because it is not one-sided, but mutually beneficial. It strengthens the stability of the region and helps in confronting its challenges; Qatar brings to the table what the United States sometimes cannot, such as contacts, communications, and negotiations with American and adversaries such as the Taliban.

Although Qatar and subsequent U.S. administrations face different challenges and sometimes have diverging interests, the two countries have maintained a constant and frank dialogue. In 2018, the two countries agreed on an annual Strategic Dialogue, engaging Qatar's leadership directly with their U.S. counterparts. The 2020 Strategic Dialogue put the capstone on one of the deepest and most extensive relations between the United States and any Gulf or Arab country.

In 1969, President Richard Nixon's administration promulgated the Nixon Doctrine, predicated on reassuring Washington's key allies of American support but also signaling that America expected its allies to fight in their own defense. The Nixon Doctrine relied on Iran and Saudi Arabia as the "twin pillars" of the Middle East's regional stability.[119]

Escalating regional events, especially the 1973 oil crisis, soon led the United States to deepen its ties directly with the region. When the United States aided Israel in the 1973 Yom Kippur War, Saudi Arabia, ostensibly a close ally, punished it with an oil embargo. Six years later, Iran, previously a "pillar of stability," underwent a revolution that transformed it into a critical threat to vital American interests. Later that year, the Soviet Union invaded Afghanistan, prompting the United States to partner with the Arab states to sponsor fundamentalist mujahideen rebels against them.

---
(119) Beinart, 2007.

Chapter 5: A Small State with a Global Influence

The United States had to redefine the security of its allies along the Arabian Peninsula's eastern shore as a vital national interest. Moreover, U.S. leaders feared that the Soviet occupation of Afghanistan posed a threat to American hegemony in the Gulf and the Indian Ocean. In response, President Jimmy Carter established the "Carter Doctrine," which stated that any attempt by any outside (i.e., Soviet) forces to gain control of the Gulf region would be regarded as an assault on the vital interests of the United States and would be opposed with military force.

The outbreak of the Iran-Iraq War in 1980 spurred the establishment of the six-nation Gulf Cooperation Council (GCC) in which Qatar played an active role working with the other Gulf states. The GCC also helped provide the political foundation for a new American security guarantee under President Ronald Reagan.

With the fall of the Berlin Wall in 1989 and the collapse of the Soviet Union in 1991, the world entered a new, unique period in global history. President George H. W. Bush spoke of a "New World Order" supported by U.S. primacy, and American hegemony faced no serious challenge from any other power. All six GCC states, given their pro-Western and anti-Communist position throughout the Cold War, regarded the new era of American primacy as an extremely positive development.

5.3. The 1991 Gulf War and U.S.-Gulf Relations

Saddam Hussein's 1990 invasion of Kuwait confronted the Arab Gulf states with their first serious security problem since the Iranian revolution. Fortunately, the U.S.-led international coalition successfully liberated the oil-rich Arabian emirate, ending a crisis with major worldwide ramifications. The ease with which U.S. troops and their allies defeated the Iraqi Army under-scored how much the balance of power in the Middle East had shifted in Washington's favor.

In the aftermath of the Gulf War, Qatar and the other GCC states worked with Washington to deepen security partnerships in the belief that the United States was uniquely positioned to defend the smaller GCC states from more powerful states in the region, such as Iraq and Iran.

Chapter 5: A Small State with a Global Influence

Relations in the Gulf, both between the GCC states and with outside powers, were still far from perfect. Qatar and Bahrain were involved in a conflict over maritime border areas and islands, a dispute that almost led to war between them in 1968. More ominously, in 1988, American-Qatari relations faced their first serious challenge. When the United States supplied Bahrain with 70 shoulder-fired "Stinger" anti-aircraft missiles, Qatar requested its own, and after the United States declined the request, bought them on the black market from the Afghan mujahideen. Furious, Washington demanded that Qatar turn over the missiles and reveal the source that had sold them. Qatar refused, prompting Congress to impose an arms embargo. Eventually, Qatar "disposed" of the missiles it obtained, but did not report their serial numbers until the early 1990s, when the two countries signed a defense agreement.[120]

The row over the Stinger missiles was serious, but after the liberation of Kuwait, Qatari-American relations deepened. On June 23, 1992, Qatar signed a defense cooperation agreement with the United States, the first defense agreement signed by Qatar outside the framework of the Gulf Cooperation Council. The agreement centered on three main issues: organizing the U.S. military presence in Qatar, defining the scope of U.S. use of Qatari military installations, and training and developing the Qatari armed forces.

The United States has also supported Qatar's moves toward political liberalization. In March 1999, Representatives Sue Kelly (RNY) and Carolyn Maloney (D-NY) headed a congressional delegation that observed Qatar's election for its Central Municipal Council. In the election's aftermath, Congress passed a resolution congratulating the State of Qatar and its citizens for their commitment to democratic ideals and women's suffrage (S.Con.Res. 14, March 4, 1999, and HCon.Res. 35, April 13, 1999).[121]

Over the following decade, the Qatari-American relationship improved dramatically. The rapid improvement in relations paralleled a deterioration in the relationship between the United States and Saudi Arabia. This deterioration was caused in part by the September 11th terrorist attacks; in the aftermath of the attacks, it

---
(120) McManus et. al., 1988.
(121) U.S. House of Representatives, 1999; U.S. Senate, 1999.

became clear that 15 of the 19 plane hijackers were Saudi nationals. Qatar condemned the attacks, declaring solidarity with the families of the victims, and supported the U.S. military operation that toppled the Taliban regime in Afghanistan in October 2001.

One high note in U.S.-Qatar relations occurred in 2003 after Saudi Arabia requested the departure of U.S. forces stationed at the Prince Sultan base in Dhahran. Despite the difficult political situation and widespread criticism of the American presence in the Gulf, Qatar offered to host the U.S. troops departing Saudi Arabia.[122] When America accepted this offer, Qatar became the home of two of the largest U.S. bases outside of U.S. territory: the As Sayliyah U.S. Army prepositioning facility and Al Udeid Air Base, which today hosts more than 11,000 American troops, about 120 combat aircraft, the U.S. Central Command (CENTCOM), the Joint Center for Air Operations, and the Space Control Combined Air and Space Operations Center (CAOC).

Bilateral defense and security cooperation between Qatar and the United States expanded further after the American-led invasion of Iraq and overthrow of Saddam Hussein's regime in 2003. The United States and Qatar concluded a Defense Cooperation Agreement that provided for U.S. access to Qatari bases, pre-positioning of United States equipment, and joint military exercises.

5.4. The Arab Spring to the Gulf Crisis (2011-2017)

During the first decade of the twenty-first century, the Gulf States, including Qatar, emerged as major players on the global stage of international policy and policymaking. The Gulf Cooperation Council countries became more active in international issues, exploiting their energy resources and capital accumulation to exert influence during the boom in oil prices between 2002 and 2008.

During the period between the influx of American troops to Qatar (2003) and the beginning of the Arab Spring (2011), Qatar adopted a political, economic, and defense approach with a high degree of independence. This independence was in part guaranteed by the presence of American troops in Qatar, giving it a high degree of security.

---

(122) BBC, 2003.

Chapter 5: A Small State with a Global Influence

Throughout its existence, Qatar has adopted an open foreign policy dependent on soft power tools, such as the media, diplomacy, education, culture, sports, tourism, economics, and humanitarian aid. The overarching goals of this policy were very simple: Qatar sought to maintain good relations with its neighbors, secure alliances with global and regional powers, and build its brand as a liberal, modern state. These goals are made explicit in Article Seven of the Qatari constitution that states the nation's foreign policy "is based on the principle of consolidating international peace and security." Qatari foreign policy relies on a set of liberal principles: encouraging the peaceful settlement of international disputes, supporting the right of peoples to self-determination, expounding non-interference in the internal affairs of states, and ensuring cooperation with peaceful nations.

Successive Qatari governments have repeatedly advocated such a policy from the mid-1990s to the present. Qatari efforts to resolve disputes in Sudan, Eritrea, Lebanon, Palestine, Somalia, and Yemen have turned Doha into a unique destination for international mediation. Many of these mediation efforts achieved positive results. Qatar facilitated the release of six Bulgarian nurses and a Palestinian doctor detained in Libya in 2007 and secured a political agreement in Lebanon in May 2008. This gave Qatar international recognition and credibility stemming from its determination to settle disputes by peaceful means. Qatar's recent mediation efforts have been relatively diverse, including both classic Track I diplomacy (as in Yemen and Lebanon) and multi-track efforts targeting political groups and civil society (as in Darfur). Similarly, Qatar has acted as both solo mediator and in partnership with such entities as the African Union, the United Nations, the Arab League, and the Gulf Cooperation Council (GCC).

From 2008 to 2012, Qatar served as an impartial broker of ten regional and international conflicts, including the Doha Agreement in the 2008 Lebanon conflict, the cease-fire agreement in Yemen in 2008, a ceasefire in the North/South Sudan conflict in 2010, the (second) Doha Agreement in the Fatah-Hamas conflict in 2012, and negotiations in conflicts in Western Sahara, Algeria, Eritrea/Ethiopia, Djibouti, and Somalia.[123]

---

(123) Barakat, 2019.

Chapter 5: A Small State with a Global Influence

With the outbreak of the Arab Spring, the Qatari leadership supported the demands of the Arab peoples, which came in the form of peaceful demonstrations against authoritarian regimes. Although the street uprisings in the "Arab Spring" succeeded in some Arab countries, such as Tunisia, they were confronted with force by entrenched regimes and counter-revolution in other Arab countries.[124]

The Qatari position in support of the Arab Spring revolutions in Egypt, Libya, and Syria coincided with that of the United States, but not without some confusion. When President Barack Obama came to power in 2009, he sought to repair the relationship with the Arab and Muslim world that President Bush had disrupted by invading both an Islamic country (Afghanistan) and an Arab country (Iraq). Obama saw this reconciliation as the easiest way to allow the United States to withdraw from Iraq and Afghanistan smoothly and without complications.

Unexpectedly, the Arab Spring's revolutions, which sought to overthrow the governments that Obama pursued better relations with, presented a serious challenge to America's new foreign policy. Although regional stability would pave the way for the smooth withdrawal of U.S. forces, America could not easily stand aside and ignore efforts to suppress peaceful uprisings seeking freedom and human dignity in Arab countries such as Tunisia, Egypt, and Yemen. Eventually, to the discomfort of the GCC states, Obama came down on the side of the protests, and Qatar formed part of the military coalition led by the United States that toppled Libyan leader Muammar Qaddafi.

Qatar saw in the Arab Spring a combination of policies designed to further participatory government in the Arab world and was heartened by what appeared to be the American administration's support of this vision. Unfortunately, U.S. policy vacillated between active intervention, as in Libya, and reluctance to commit significant armed force, as in Syria. Qatar found itself trying to balance various regional power centers, such as Turkey and Saudi Arabia, in these conflicts. As a consequence, Qatar became more cautious in its involvement.

---

(124) Barakat, 2014.

Chapter 5: A Small State with a Global Influence

The ascent of Sheikh Tamim bin Hamad Al Thani to the Qatari throne in 2013 changed the way Qatar's diplomacy dealt with the consequences of the Arab Spring. The new Qatari strategic approach reflected the writings of Joseph Nye, who outlined the concept of "smart power," which blends soft and hard forces while preserving the principles of the country's foreign policy.[125]

Sheikh Tamim's first visit to Washington took place on February 24, 2015, to assert the independence of Qatar's foreign policy without compromising its alliance with the United States. In an article entitled "Qatar's Message to Obama" published in the New York Times on February 24, Sheikh Tamim wrote that "military solutions are insufficient to defeat terrorism and confront the strategic challenges facing the Middle East and the world." The emir stressed the need to assess this phenomenon within its social, economic, and political contexts, allowing it to be addressed from its roots.

Sheikh Tamim pointed out that "this war requires political leaders to have the courage to negotiate pluralistic and comprehensive solutions to regional conflicts, in addition to providing accountability for tyrants." He concluded his article by warning that "if the dreams of young people in the Arab world for freedom, justice and economic security are not realized ... extremism will reproduce itself." During this visit, President Obama recognized the importance of the role played by Qatar in the international coalition in the war against the Islamic State (ISIS), stressing that the relationship would "remain solid, close and mutually beneficial."[126]

Under Sheikh Tamim, the new Qatari leadership has adopted a policy that keeps the door open for dialogue with all parties in the Arab world, while stressing the urgent necessity of not excluding any force from the political scene. This position has fueled disputes with some neighboring countries that prefer to violently confront some of their Islamist movements and reformists. For this reason, three GCC countries—Saudi Arabia, the UAE, and Bahrain—withdrew their ambassadors from Doha on March 5, 2014, creating the largest challenge that Qatar's leadership had yet faced in the modern era. This crisis, unprecedented in the GCC's prior history, demonstrated the depth of the dispute between the Gulf states.

---

(125) Nye, 2005.
(126) Al Thani, 2015.

Although the 2014 crisis was soon contained, it returned in 2017 with greater force and with the additional participation of Egypt. The 2017 crisis became the worst intra-GCC dispute since the establishment of the organization in 1981; there had never been a boycott or embargo of a GCC member state prior to 2017, or since. Qatar's neighbors closed all land and sea ports and prohibited transit of their territory, airspace, and waters. In addition, the neighboring countries banned Qatari citizens from traveling to or through the four boycotting states and ordered the immediate departure of Qatari residents and visitors within two weeks.[127]

The crisis deeply concerned the United States, which had come to rely on a politically united Gulf. Initially, President Trump had believed the accusations leveled at Qatar and joined in the criticism. Very quickly he came to realize that the accusations had no factual basis. Then-Secretary of State Rex Tillerson made more than twenty phone calls trying to resolve the crisis. He also supported Kuwaiti mediation efforts to reach a diplomatic solution and maintain the unity of the GCC. Then-Secretary of Defense James Mattis also emphasized the security and strategic partnership between the United States and Qatar.[128]

Moreover, American officials had cause to doubt the motives of the blockading countries. Despite the accusations made against Qatar that focused largely on the peninsular nation's supposed political and financial support for terrorism, State Department spokeswoman Heather Nauert also questioned whether the blockade was really based on concerns about Qatar's support for terrorism—or if it related to old problems and grievances between the GCC states.

The position of the chairman of the Senate Foreign Relations Committee, Bob Corker Jr., was the strictest when he announced that he would block arms sales to all the GCC countries until they resolved the dispute with Qatar. Former CIA Director David Petraeus, quoted by the French newspaper Journal du Dimanche, commented on the accusations that Doha supported terrorist organizations by noting that Qatar

---

(127) Nephew, 2020.
(128) CNBC, 2017.

had hosted Taliban delegations and funded Hamas-affiliated humanitarian operations in Gaza, but with the knowledge and at the request of the U.S. government.[129]

5.5. U.S. Realignment After the Blockade

In the wake of the June 2017 Gulf crisis, Qatar strengthened its relations with its American strategic ally. It worked to draw a road map for the future of bilateral relations between the two countries, including the inclusion of Al Udeid in the list of permanent military bases of the United States.

At the onset of the 2017 Gulf crisis, Qatar's neighbors insisted that the United States depart from its bases in Qatar. The Pentagon refused; it announced that American forces had no plan to leave Al Udeid Air Base, confirming Washington's commitment to military and security relations with Doha.

Department of Defense spokespeople at the time noted the importance of Al Udeid in America's Middle East mission and the hospitality of the Qatari government. "Qatar has been and remains an exceptional partner, and this base from which we operate is a great base. The Central Command has no intention of moving to any other place," said Maj. Gen. B. Chance Saltzman, Deputy Commander of U.S. Air Force at the U.S. Central Command. The U.S. Department of Defense spokesperson for Central Command, Rebecca Rebarich, also denied the existence of any plan for American withdrawal from Al Udeid.

Paradoxically, the 2017 blockade of Qatar by its neighbors appears to have strengthened the Qatar-American strategic partnership. The summit meeting that brought together President Trump and Sheikh Tamim in April 2018 at the White House represented a milestone in the relations between the two countries. It also led to a gradual shift in Trump's stance towards the Gulf crisis, following conflicting statements. At the time of their 2018 meeting, President Trump told Sheikh Tamim that he had come to realize that the countries besieging Qatar were the ones that were hindering finding a solution to the Gulf crisis. Trump praised Sheikh Tamim, describing their relationship as a "long friendship." He also stressed his commitment to solving the Gulf crisis "very quickly," saying that U.S. relations with Qatar were not confined to the Gulf crisis but included "mutual trade and many other issues. And we have excellent relations."

---
(129) Qatar Tribune, 2017.

Chapter 5: A Small State with a Global Influence

The summit meeting between the two leaders opened the U.S.-Qatar Strategic Dialogue in late January 2018, which took place in Washington under the auspices of the foreign and defense ministers of the two countries.[130] That dialogue was the first of its kind between the two countries. They agreed to follow up with an annual strategic dialogue forum. At the time, the two countries believed that the institutionalization of an annual dialogue would demonstrate the strength of the bilateral relations between them and provide "foundations for a common future vision for their strategic partnership."

This agreement showed that Qatar had successfully managed to circumvent the attempts of the blockading countries to isolate it from the United States. However, the most important outcome of the U.S.-Qatar strategic dialogue at the time was the official announcement of the United States' "willingness to work with Qatar to deter and confront any external threat to the territorial integrity of the State of Qatar, in contravention of the Charter of the United Nations"—incontestably a reprimand to the blockading countries.

According to a congressional report, the second round of the strategic dialogue resulted in the signing of a memorandum of understanding on "improving and expanding Al Udeid Base." The report emphasized that relations had witnessed a qualitative shift since Washington and Doha began the work of "strategic dialogue" in January 2018.[131] It quotes U.S. military officials as asserting that Qatar represented "a long friendship and military partnership that supports stability in the Middle East and supports NATO's mission in Afghanistan."

The joint statement issued after the September 2020 U.S.-Qatar Strategic Dialogue in Washington put the capstone on the relationship. The 11-page document outlines a broad series of social, cultural, and economic projects, in addition to further enhancing the strategic diplomatic relationship between the two countries.

To improve its own security position, Qatar also began a renewed effort to purchase modern military equipment from the United States. The first major Qatari arms deal with the United States had been negotiated in 2012. The $6.6 billion deal included Apache

---

(130) CBS, 2018.
(131) Congressional Record, 2019.

Chapter 5: A Small State with a Global Influence

AH64 attack helicopters, UH-60 Black Hawk helicopters, and MH-60 hovercraft. In April 2018, the U.S. State Department announced more arms deals with Qatar, a $12 billion agreement to purchase F-15 fighters, and the procurement of guided missiles for the Apaches valued at $300 million. These agreements demonstrated Qatar's affirmation of its long-term commitment to work with its ally, the United States.

Despite the Gulf crisis, the United States expanded military ties with Qatar. In March 2018, the State Department approved a $200 million deal to establish an Air Operations Center at Al Udeid. During the 2018 Qatari-American strategic dialogue, Qatar announced that it was financing the expansion of bases to facilitate a permanent U.S. military presence in Qatar. This project included the construction of 200 new housing units for U.S. personnel and their families. The two countries are also in the process of establishing a naval base for hosting U.S. Navy operations, should it choose to operate from Qatar. In July 2019, Qatar opened the new Al-Daayen Naval Base 30 km north of Doha. According to Admiral Jim Malloy, Commander of the U.S. Navy's 5th Fleet, this base will increase the potential for maritime cooperation.[132] The Qatari Armed Forces also signed agreements to purchase an air defense system from Raytheon and a logistics maintenance system from Boeing.[133]

Military and security cooperation between Qatar and the United States has received praise not only from the U.S. government but from legislators, researchers, and other influential groups. A congressional report praised the importance of the strategic dialogue between the United States and Qatar and supported further bilateral cooperation between the two countries. The congressional report indicated that Qatari-American military relations had grown steadily since the nations signed their defense cooperation treaty in 1992 and put special emphasis on Qatar's hosting of Al Udeid.

5.6. Cooperation on Counter-Terrorism

Even before the Gulf crisis began in 2017, Qatar was able, despite the obvious imbalance in size and power, to prove itself indispensable to the United States. Since the crisis, the two nations' cooperation has expanded in many fields. The United States depends on Qatar to play an independent role and negotiate on its behalf. For example,

---
(132) AFP, 2019.
(133) Tapestry Solutions, 2018.

Chapter 5: A Small State with a Global Influence

even before U.S.-Taliban negotiations began in earnest, and when the Taliban was designated as a terrorist organization, Doha allowed the Taliban in 2013 to open an office in Qatar, at the request of the U.S. government, to provide a venue for negotiations.

The negotiations took painstaking and arduous efforts from both parties. Washington dispatched Zalmay Khalilzad, the U.S. Special Envoy for Afghanistan, while the Taliban sent their political bureau chief and deputy leader of the movement, Mullah Abdul Ghani Berdar. The U.S.-Taliban dialogue eventually resulted in the signing of an agreement on February 29, 2020, between the United States and the Taliban. The agreement provided for the withdrawal of 12,000 U.S. troops from Afghanistan in exchange for security guarantees, in addition to the Taliban's commitment to dialogue to bring about peace.[134]

Qatar's openness to engage with groups that the United States opposes and classifies as terrorists, such as Hamas, or groups it is actively at war against, such as the Taliban, has made Qatar a unique and distinctive mediator. Moreover, the ability to talk to those who other states refuse to communicate with actually benefits its relationship with Washington.[135]

Relations between Qatar and the United States have made great strides since the 1990s on the issue of counter-terrorism. The two sides succeeded in establishing a dialogue to strengthen the fight against terrorism, stop its financing, search for the roots behind the spread of the phenomenon, and address its causes. Less than a month and a half after the outbreak of the Gulf crisis, Qatar and the United States signed a "Memorandum of Understanding for cooperation in the fight against the financing of terrorism" establishing security and financial intelligence cooperation between the two countries to combat terrorism.

The Memorandum of Understanding, which was concluded after the countries of the Gulf Cooperation Council signed an agreement to combat terrorism with President Trump in May 2017, is the first and only one of its kind between any country in the GCC and the United States. It ensures increased cooperation between

---
(134) Zucchino, 2019.
(135) Qatar Tribune, 2017.

Chapter 5: A Small State with a Global Influence

military forces and in intelligence cooperation. The Memorandum gives the U.S. Treasury the opportunity to work closely with the Qatari government to help monitor suspected terrorist financing activities. It makes Qatar an active member of the Anti-ISIS Financial Group, aimed at reducing terrorist groups' financial capabilities.[136]

Qatar's efforts in the field of counter-terrorism stem from its belief that terrorism is a threat to the entire world, as expressed by Qatari diplomacy in all regional and international forums and official state speeches. The relations that link Qatar with the United States, whether political, economic, or cultural, play a crucial role in combating terrorism and ensuring lasting peace, regionally and internationally. However, Qatar believes that military solutions alone are not sufficient to defeat terrorism and address its causes. Hence, it is working with partners to contribute to diplomatic solutions to long-term conflicts that cause persistent mistrust and fuel the frustration that breeds extremism and terrorism. Qatar is also one of the founders and major contributors to the Global Fund for Community Participation and Resilience, which aims to enhance resilience in the face of violent extremist ideologies. Qatar's leadership believes that anti-terrorism efforts should not be limited to defense and security. Terrorism must also be combated through strengthening the rule of law, promoting citizenship rights, establishing a culture of reconciliation and coexistence, rejecting sectarianism, and tackling the challenges of poverty and unemployment.

In order to support efforts to combat terrorism and extremism, Doha hosts several international conferences on combating terrorism and dealing with terrorists. In September 2019, Doha hosted an international conference to study the causes of extremism, with the participation of a group of international experts, scholars, and decision-makers from around the world. This event, the first of its kind in the Middle East, included sessions on the role of evidence-based policy in combating extremism, assessing risk factors, examining ways to monitor and combat it, researching its resilience, and introducing new approaches to measuring it. In 2018, Doha hosted another international conference to discuss ways to deal with the return of

---

(136) Finn, 2017.

foreign fighters from conflict areas and how to rehabilitate them.

Qatar's effective role in combating terrorism has been noted in Washington. The U.S. government has repeatedly praised Qatar's efforts to combat terrorism, noting its satisfaction with Qatar's implementation of the Anti-Terrorist Financing Agreement and cooperation in other ways. The November 2019 session of the Third U.S.-Qatar Strategic Dialogue took the partnership's most serious steps towards strengthening the fight against terrorism. In recognition of its efforts to mediate an end to the war in Afghanistan and stamp out terrorism, the Biden administration designated Qatar a "major non-NATO ally" on January 31, 2022.

On the international level, Qatar is a founding member of the Global Forum for Combating Terrorism, which coordinates efforts with 30 different countries, including France, Britain, Germany, Canada, and the United States. Qatar is also an active member of the Terrorist Financing Targeting Center that includes all the states of the GCC and the United States and aims to confront the new and evolving risks of terrorist financing.

In December 2018, Qatar and the United Nations Office for Counter-Terrorism (UNOCT) signed an agreement to establish a United Nations counter-terrorism office in Doha. In the aftermath, in March 2019, the State of Qatar and the United Nations Office for Counter-Terrorism held the first strategic dialogue at the United Nations Headquarters.[137]

Finally, in September 2019, the United Nations Office for Combating Terrorism and the International Sports Security Center signed an agreement aimed at strengthening cooperation on preventing and combating terrorism, especially with regard to protecting major sporting events—a topic made particularly relevant with the upcoming 2022 World Cup.[138]

---

(137) UNOCT, 2020.
(138) Ibid.

Chapter 5: A Small State with a Global Influence

5.7. Qatar's Crucial Help in the U.S. Withdrawal from Afghanistan

Qatar played a prominent role in negotiations during America's 20-year war in Afghanistan. The country hosted the talks between the United States and the Taliban in Doha, which led to the U.S. withdrawal from the country beginning on May 1, 2021. Doha also hosted negotiations between the Taliban and the internationally recognized government of President Ashraf Ghani, prior to that government's abrupt capitulation in August 2021.

Although the Taliban's takeover of Afghanistan in August took most outside observers by surprise, the chaos that followed provided Qatar with an additional opportunity to burnish its humanitarian credentials and display its key regional role to both the Taliban and the United States. After the fall of Kabul, the U.S. sought assistance from Qatar to help evacuate tens of thousands of Afghans via an "air bridge" between Kabul's Hamid Karzai International Airport and Qatar's Al Udeid Air Base. These efforts enjoyed both the support of the United States and the acquiescence of the Taliban, and Qatar was praised by U.S. Secretary of State Antony Blinken for its major role in the evacuations. Doha also played a role in efforts to stabilize the situation within Kabul after the U.S. withdrawal. It provided aid to international agencies and assisted media outlets with on-the-ground reporting. Of the more than 100,000 evacuees from Afghanistan, the majority traveled via Qatari planes, and the New York Times mentioned that Doha had helped in evacuating journalists from the Washington Post, the New York Times, the Guardian, and other Western newspapers.[139]

Qatari Deputy Prime Minister and Foreign Minister Mohammad bin Abdulrahman Al Thani mentioned in the fourth annual Qatari-American Strategic Dialogue that the Qatari-American relationship had become stronger after the two nations' cooperation during the evacuation process.[140] Both countries worked around the clock to evacuate 122,000 individuals, including American citizens, female students, Afghan interpreters, civil servants working for the Ghani administration, and journalists and their families from around the world.

---

(139) Grynbaum, M., Hsu, T., and Robertson, K., 2021.
(140) U.S. Department of State, 2021.

Chapter 5: A Small State with a Global Influence

The Qatari military assisted in the evacuation through hundreds of soldiers and military aircraft. Even the Qatari ambassador to Afghanistan helped to assist civilian convoys through Taliban checkpoints in Kabul, until they had reached the airport.[141] At the same time, the Qataris hosted tens of thousands of Afghan refugees at a time within the Al Udeid air base, a significant challenge considering the large number of refugees and the complexity of the operation.

At Al Udeid, Qatar established a field hospital and shelters to host thousands of Afghan refugees until the United States and other host countries could process their applications for asylum. The Qatari army helped to distribute 50,000 meals a day, and several agencies of Qatar's civil society also provided aid. The country's airlines provided ten planes to help transport refugees from Doha to other countries.[142]

At the same time that Doha assisted the United States with the evacuation, it also helped the Taliban maintain order in Kabul. Owing to extensive damage to the Kabul airport during the evacuation, the Taliban-led interim government asked Doha to help restore and operate it once the evacuation had concluded.[143] Returning the airport to use also became an important matter for the United States, as many American and European citizens continued to await evacuation in Kabul. Given their long opposition to the Taliban and uncertainty over the safety of Kabul, the U.S., the Netherlands, the UK and the EU decided to halt their diplomatic work in Kabul and move their embassies to Doha.

President Joe Biden publicly thanked the Emir of Qatar for helping in the evacuation and for helping with the peace and reconciliation efforts in Afghanistan. In a phone call between Biden and the Emir, the president noted that the Kabul airlift had been the largest airlift in history, and its success "would not have been possible without the early support from Qatar."[144]

---

(141) Al Jazeera, 2021.
(142) Ibid.
(143) Reuters, 2021.
(144) White House, 2021.

Chapter 5: A Small State with a Global Influence

Senator Chris Coons, a member of the Senate Foreign Relations Committee, thanked the Qatari Emir and the Foreign Minister for providing a safe corridor for Americans and Afghans through Qatar to the United States. In a tweet, Coons thanked both men and the Qatari nation for "extending safe passage to Americans and Afghan nationals from Afghanistan through Qatar to the U.S.," noting that he was working with other high-level U.S. officials to resettle the refugees as quickly as possible.[145]

5.8. Conclusion

The U.S.-Qatari security relationship has progressed dramatically since the 1998 crisis over Stinger missile sales to Bahrain. Today, Qatar and the United States enjoy deep strategic ties in defense, security, counter-terrorism, and conflict resolution.

In January 2021, Qatar and Saudi Arabia agreed to end the blockade, an agreement that the UAE and Bahrain grudgingly joined. This agreement, negotiated at the 2021 GCC summit at Al-Ula, ended the most serious diplomatic crisis in the GCC's history. American diplomacy played an important role in achieving this resolution.

---

(145) Coons, 2021.

Photography

Qatari troops during the 1991 Gulf War.

President George W. Bush visiting American troops at Al Udeid Air Base in Doha, 2003.

Emir Tamim Al-Thani (right) and President Barack Obama (center) at Camp David.

Congressional delegation, including Speaker Pelosi, visiting Al Udeid Air Base.

A display of American aircraft operated by the Qatari Air Force.

Sheikh Tamim addressing the opening session of the UN General Assembly.

Photography

U.S. Secretary of State and Qatari Foreign Minister signing agreements.

U.S. and Qatari ministers of defense and foreign affairs meeting.

A military cooperation agreement between Qatar and the United States, 2021.

Qatari National Day celebration parade.

Ivanka Trump visits Al Udeid in 2019.

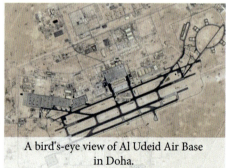
A bird's-eye view of Al Udeid Air Base in Doha.

Chapter 6
The Evolution of Qatar's Education System

6.1. Introduction

Qatar has emerged as a pioneer in the field of modern education and higher education in the Middle East and has achieved advanced positions in international assessments in this regard for decades. Development in Qatar's education sector started early; the nation's first elementary and secondary schools were established in the 1950s and 1960s, well before its independence. The Qatari institutions also educated many of the most important personalities of that generation in the entire Gulf.

At the time, the Gulf sheikhdoms lacked any tertiary educational institutions—a situation that persisted when the British departed in 1971. Wealthy Qataris sent their children abroad for higher education, and many traveled to other Arab countries such as Egypt, Lebanon, and Iraq. Others went to Western countries such as Britain and the United Sates; anecdotal accounts indicate that Qataris first began to study in America in the early 1970s.[146]

As a result of continuous and growing educational scholarships over the past years, there was a boom in this field. In the first decade of the twenty-first century, Qatar and the United States developed a unique relationship in building and strengthening higher education, a relationship that other Gulf and Arab countries now seek to imitate and learn from.

---

(146) Personal interviews with Qataris, including former Minister of Energy Abdullah al Attiyah, who attended the University in Michigan in the early 1970s.

Chapter 6: The Evolution of Qatar's Education System

The Qatari-American experiment, in cooperation with American universities, resulted in the creation of the pioneering Education City in Doha. It has nurtured and impacted the larger geopolitical, cultural, and humanitarian relations between the two countries and has revolutionized American higher education's outreach abroad.

6.2. Early Education in Qatar

Qatar had no formal education system prior to the discovery of oil. Despite this, in less than a century, Qatari society has moved to the front ranks of the Gulf countries that adopt and support educational advances and initiatives.

Until the 1950s, Qatari education offered only traditional methods of learning, like other Gulf states, that emphasized memorization of the Quran and the learning of Arabic (locally known as Katateeb). However, one of the first government departments was the Ministry of Education in 1956, created to oversee the growth of a primary and secondary schooling system as well as vocational training courses. This dramatic change was made possible by the early foundations of Qatar's modern education system—foundations that helped the small nation establish an institutionalized education system that quickly became among the best in the region.[147]

The first recorded modern school in Qatar, the Al-Atharyyah School, opened in 1913. A number of prominent families sent their children to the school from other Gulf countries before it closed in 1938.[148] Another elementary school for boys, Al-Eslah' Al-Hamadiyyah in Doha, opened as a private school in 1948 with one teacher and 50 pupils. In its first year, it attracted 30 students from Sharjah. Al-Eslah' Al-Hamadiyyah did not receive government support until 1950 when education became free for the national population, and by 1952 it had grown rapidly to six teachers and 240 boys.

Other schools had opened by 1954, and in 1956, Qatar opened its first school for girls and launched its first secondary school. That secondary school, Al-Doha Secondary School

---
(147) Potter, 2018.
(148) Nasser, 2017.

Chapter 6: The Evolution of Qatar's Education System

(Madrasat Al-Dawh'ah Al-Thanawiyyah), established Qatar as an early regional hub for education.[149]

Prominent Al-Doha Secondary School graduates include Ahmed Khalifa Al-Suwaidi, the first UAE foreign minister; Rashid Abdullah Al-Nuaimi, UAE foreign minister at the time of the formation of the GCC; and Mana' Saeed Al-Otayba, the UAE's first oil minister and father of the current UAE Ambassador in Washington.[150] This early stake in education laid the ground for today's Qatar as the preeminent educational hub in the region.

The oil boom and its ramifications fundamentally transformed all aspects of Qatari society. State-provided social welfare benefits created new opportunities for citizens and residents, as well as a high-quality educational system that provided privileges and a new stream of teachers and students from different nations and ages.

In the 1970s and 1980s, Qatari leadership diligently worked on eliminating illiteracy and providing comprehensive education for all citizens and residents, although quantity and speed took priority over the actual quality of education. Almost all of the first generation of teachers were Arab expatriates from Palestine, Jordan, and Egypt, and they played a significant role in the design of early textbooks and curricula. At that point, however, the country focused on the overall vision more than setting goals related to a period of time that could be measured and adjusting its outputs, especially in the higher education sector.[151]

Qatar's first tertiary educational institution, Qatar University, opened its doors in 1973 as a teachers' college with an entering class of 93 women and 57 men. By 1977, it had four new colleges: Education, Humanities & Social Sciences, Sharia Law and Islamic Studies, and Science. Since then, Qatar University has grown exponentially. It has added faculties in Business and Economics, Engineering, Law, Pharmacy, Health Science, Medicine, and, most recently, the College of Dental Medicine. It now boasts a total of nearly 8,000 students, and a 13:1 student-teacher ratio. To date, there are more than 30,000 alumni.

---

(149) Al-Maadheed, 2017.
(150) Co-author's conversations.
(151) Nasser, 2017.

Chapter 6: The Evolution of Qatar's Education System

By the 1990s, greater numbers of Qatari men and women entered the workforce and started looking for jobs beyond the public sector. The government began to show mounting concern over the quality of Qatar's education system and its inability to prepare young Qataris for a changing and more competitive labor market. There was a growing awareness of the educational sector's importance to Qatar's future and the prospects for developing a knowledge-based economy that could free Qatar of its dependence on hydrocarbons. A first step was taken in 1996 with the formation of a committee of experts from government ministries and Qatar University to evaluate the existing system of primary and secondary education and identify issues of concern and areas for improvement.

The committee report identified deficiencies in physical infrastructure and the shortage of qualified teachers.[152] The emir, Sheikh Hamad, outlined a vision of progress for the twenty-first century in an address to the Qatar University graduating class of 1998.

To deal with shortfalls in Qatar's K-12 education system and to bring it up to par with systems elsewhere, Doha sought assistance from the RAND Corporation, an American consulting group. Tasked with analyzing the existing education system and suggesting alternatives, RAND drew up a report in 2001 entitled "Education for a New Era." It provided Qataris with a range of recommendations and options, including improving teaching quality in order to boost student achievement.[153]

The report noted that Qatari schools placed too great an emphasis on traditional rote learning. Qatari schools had also failed to keep pace with rapid developments in information technology and updated methods of learning elsewhere in the world. Other issues included high student-to-teacher ratios, overcrowded classrooms, low teacher and administrator pay, and lack of incentives that could induce high-achieving Qataris to train as teachers and enter the classroom. RAND's studies concluded that the country's education system lacked a coherent vision, and Qatari schools' organizational structures were too hierarchical.

---

(152) Al-Maadheed, 2017.
(153) Nasser, 2017.

After 1995, Emir Hamad, working with his wife, Sheikha Mozah bint Nasr, determined to improve the country's education system. Sheikh Hamad told the co-author, at the presentation of his credentials as the American ambassador to Doha, that his top priority as emir was to improve Qatar's education system, confiding that he wished to be remembered as the "education Emir."[154]

6.3. New Directions in Education

Early in the twenty-first century, Qatar began implementing some of the changes recommended by RAND, including the implementation of a standards-based system and the establishment of the Supreme Education Council (SEC) to replace the Ministry of Education. The SEC was comprised of three organizations: the Education Institute, the Evaluation Institute, and the Higher Education Institute.

RAND had proposed three options for Qatar: (1) establishing government-financed "independent schools" that would independently design their own curriculum and teaching methods with only minimal government intervention; (2) introducing a voucher system that would enable parents to select private schools for their children; and (3) reforming Qatar's centralized education system while maintaining government oversight. Officials in Doha ultimately picked the first choice, and the Independent School System came into being. As David B. Roberts at King's College London explains, "When offered several choices of how to reform Qatar's schools by the U.S. think-tank RAND Corporation, Qatar's leadership chose the option with the deepest changes explicitly modeled on the U.S. school system."[155]

This decision made Qatar distinct from its neighbors and peers in the Arabian Gulf and the Arab world. Middle Eastern governments typically control education systems closely, keeping them in the public sector. By looking to the private sector to improve the quality of education for Qatari society, the Qatari leadership was making a bold move that it believed was necessary for guaranteeing results and educational outputs. The process of converting Qatari public schools into the Independent School System began in 2004 on an incremental schedule. Both systems operated in parallel until all schools completed the transition in 2010.

---

(154) Author personal Interview December 1995.
(155) Roberts, 2017.

Chapter 6: The Evolution of Qatar's Education System

As Qatar's school system began changing in line with RAND's recommendations, important changes occurred in the curricula, with a greater focus on developing performance standards in Arabic, English, mathematics, and science. Teachers were given greater autonomy in terms of selecting material for the curricula, as long as it met national standards.[156] The educational reforms provoked a measure of local resistance due to both religious and societal concerns that the new system had been imposed externally rather than growing organically from Qatari society. A robust debate ensued in the Qatari media and public space about the changes. The exclusion of some Islamic Studies courses left some in Qatar fearful that the Independent Schools would not teach this subject, and society would suffer as a consequence. In response, the SEC required all Independent Schools to add this subject to the four core subjects.

By 2010, the Ministry had gradually converted all its public schools into Independent Schools. Following RAND's recommendations, the SEC also moved to improve teachers' skills. Until then, teachers in Qatar had mainly taught in Arabic. When the Independent Schools introduced English as a language of study, they found that many teachers lacked the linguistic qualifications. To address this challenge, the SEC engaged many foreign educational companies, also referred to as the School Support Organizations (SSOs).

The major focus of the SSOs' work was to assist Qatar's schools in implementing standards. As Nasser wrote,

"The goal was to reach the point where teachers could read the standards, group them for the appropriate unit or lesson, identify the appropriateness of the standard for grade and age level, write objectives aligned with the standards according to content, identify the cognitive level related to the objectives, develop the knowledge and skills targeted in the objectives and assess the content corresponding to the curriculum."[157]

During this time, the SSOs also used internal and external expertise to implement new teaching methods that were increasingly oriented toward students increasing their educational achievements. The Independent Schools had the autonomy to hire their own staff and develop in ways they saw fit, while the SEC supported them

---
(156) Brewer et. al., 2007.
(157) Author personal Interview December 1995.

by providing teacher-training programs that covered a host of topics, including curriculum standards, student-centered teaching, and enhancement of skills. The SSOs' efforts to strengthen Qatar's education system by training coordinators and teachers from the country's Independent Schools paid off, as those who received the training quickly became qualified to train new teachers.[158]

The College of Education at Qatar University, where most teachers in Qatar receive their training, also played a major role by establishing the Center for Teaching and Research Development. This center later became the Teacher Development Center and served the education system in Qatar by providing various forms of support and advice to schools.

In late 2010, faculty members from the State of Texas Education Research Center at Texas A&M University and the College of Education at Qatar University conducted a joint research group to better understand the requirements of the teaching profession in Qatar. The two institutions studied 29 of Qatar's Independent Schools. They concluded that although teachers had participated in countless workshops aimed at advancing their professional development, they required further improvement in many areas. The researchers recommended making teachers' training more practical and less theoretical. The researchers also concluded that more workshops and exchange experiences with other educational institutions would benefit the development of the Independent Schools. The Qatari government eventually moved away from the RAND model after 2011, building on the experience of the Independent Schools to re-establish a revamped and expanded public school system.

Private schools have also played an important role in the Qatari education sector. Sponsored by the British Embassy, Doha College was established in 1980. Not to be outdone, the American Embassy sponsored the American Community School (ACS) in 1988. Both the Doha College and the American Community School have student bodies that comprise more than 75 nationalities, including many Qataris, reflecting the extraordinary diversity of Qatar's residents. Other embassy-associated schools include two French lycée schools, the German International School, the Qatar

---
(158) Roberts, 2017.

Canadian School, the Japan School of Doha, the Qatar Turkish School, and the Doha Modern Indian School.

Several new fully private schools also opened their doors in Qatar. Qatar Academy opened in 1995 and grew into a group of five private schools administered by the Qatar Foundation that offered the International Baccalaureate program to their students. More private schools followed suit, including the Doha British School, which offered a choice of the International Baccalaureate and A Levels, and the Doha Academy, launched in 2000 as a Muslim institute of education with three campuses across Qatar.

6.4. American Universities and Education City

During the 1970s and 1980s, the Qatari government gave scholarships to students who wished to study abroad seeking educational opportunities beyond the scope of Qatar University. In 1996, however, Sheikh Hamid and Sheikha Mozah conceived a completely new approach to bringing higher education to Qatar by launching the ambitious Education City project, supervised and managed by the Qatar Foundation for Education, Science and Community Development (Qatar Foundation, or QF).

QF, established in 1995, has gained a global reputation for its educational initiatives at all levels of learning. The emergence, subsequent expansion, and successes of Education City, as reported in the Washington Post in 2015, reflected "rapid globalization in academia" as the city provides "an optimistic vision of social progress in the Middle East."[159] In addition to success in non-science and energy sectors such as finance, media, culture, and art, coupled with a unique strategy for global diplomacy, Qatar's strategic position in the field of education helped the country create a truly international image.

The Qatar Foundation had studied the limited success of the neighboring countries that had opened "American" schools and universities. These "American" schools had failed to provide education at the level expected of American and other foreign universities. The schools suffered from being established by local businesses as for-profit ventures. Although associated at their establishment with various American universities, the business owners quickly diluted the

---
(159) Anderson, 2015.

"American" component because it was too expensive. The American partner schools also declined to give students transcripts or degrees from the home school because they had little or no control over the educational process in the Arab partner country. Qatari leadership recognized that the domestic for-profit model had little success.

For this reason, invitations were sent to prestigious American universities to establish branch campuses in Qatar. The Qatari vision called for a branch campus that had a "seamless relationship" with the home school. This would require the sending university to fully establish the campus, staff it with home school faculty, provide a home school curriculum and rules, and issue home campus transcripts and diplomas.

With this model, students, through their academic achievement, would have the same system as the home school under the same rigorous competitive rules. Should they move from the Qatar campus to the home campus or vice versa, they would not be classified as "transfer" students with all the attendant requirements but as students moving from one internal college to another.

Qatar offered to fund the project on a "cost plus" basis. The sending school would provide an operational budget (including home school overhead). Qatar Foundation would reimburse the costs, plus a fee to be negotiated, and build and operate the physical facilities. Universities would have complete control over new student admissions, although fully-qualified Qatari citizen applicants would be admitted and never wait-listed. Additionally, Qatar Foundation agreed not to interfere in any academic activity, censor the curriculum, or impose any other requirements (such as gender-segregated classes) as long as the school and its staff abided by Qatari law.

On this basis, QF initiated negotiations with a number of top-ranking American schools, but all failed to come to a conclusion that satisfied both parties, as Qatar demanded an educational standard identical to that of the home school. Achieving that standard across the entire university would require sending tenured faculty. QF realized that the incentives required to attract tenured faculty in one discipline would not attract tenured faculty in another; for in-stance, the requirements of a tenured professor of engineering would be

Chapter 6: The Evolution of Qatar's Education System

quite different than for one of medicine.[160] No one comprehensive contract could satisfy all tenured faculty.

In 2000, QF changed the direction of its search and concentrated on bringing to Qatar one outstanding school from each university. Qatar Foundation soon signed a series of agreements with six distinct schools of six American universities. The first, Virginia Commonwealth University (School of Design Arts) had operated an affiliate in Qatar since 1998. Later, five other U.S.-based universities joined: Weill Cornell Medical College (2001); The Texas A&M University College of Engineering (2003); Carnegie Mellon University School of Information Technology (2004); Georgetown University School of Foreign Service (2005); and Northwestern University's School of Journalism (2008). In addition to the American branch campuses, Canada's College of the North Atlantic opened its Technical College, followed by the renowned French business school HEC Paris that opened a branch at Education City in 2010, as did University College London (UCL), which opened UCL School of Archaeology Qatar the same year.[161]

Qatar's model in educational investment differed from the models followed by other regional countries in bringing American universities to the region. New York University, for example, established a campus in Abu Dhabi in 2009 on a different single-school model with a less integrated relationship with the home campus.

Qatar believes that its model of partnerships with multiple American universities will better provide the Gulf country with access to each field of expertise and excellence in teaching and research. For example, Carnegie Mellon University is well-known for its programs in computer science and business administration, Cornell University has provided a strong program in medicine, Virginia Commonwealth University has offered excellent fine arts, and a generation of Qatari diplomats and civil servants have been trained at the Georgetown campus. Notwithstanding their diversity, American university branches in Education City have also worked closely together over time to strengthen their collaboration in numerous ways, offering joint courses and boosting the percentage of Qatari students.[162]

---

(160) Author's personal interview.
(161) Author's personal interviews, 1998 - 2002.
(162) The Peninsula, 2019.

Chapter 6: The Evolution of Qatar's Education System

Situated on a 14-square-kilometer tract of land on the outskirts of Doha, Education City has since become one of the most recognizable features of modern Qatar with its distinctive architecture, especially the open book-shaped Qatar National Library, inaugurated in 2018. The architecture of the campuses, lawns, and public spaces of the City have become symbols of Qatar's commitment to higher education and lifelong learning. Speaking in the United States in 2004, Sheikha Mozah bint Nasser, the driving force behind the project, described Education City as "an engine of change for Qatar."[163]

Two other developments in the 2000s that helped in supporting scientific research—the Qatar Science and Technology Park and the Qatar National Research Fund—played significant roles in deepening the knowledge economy infrastructure in Qatar and linking it with partners around the world. By laying the basis for international research partnerships with local Qatari and Qatar-based institutions, both initiatives have contributed to a rapid expansion in the production of scholarly and scientific output.

The Qatar Science and Technology Park (QSTP) opened in 2009. The Park has since turned into a regional hub for technology companies and local startups, and it has supported the creation of research and development networks that link Qatar to the international knowledge ecosystem. By providing financial and human resources for business incubation, mentorship, and training, the QSTP has provided practical assistance enabling Qatari and Qatar-based companies to emerge and grow.

The Qatar National Research Fund (QNRF) was established in 2006 to channel support to academic research and build bridges between Qatari and Qatar-based institutions and international partners. Through its annual National Priorities Research Program funding cycle, the QNRF has created and strengthened links that connect Qatar to worldwide networks of research and scholarship.

A number of renowned American and British think tanks—notably the Brookings Institution, the Royal United Service Institute (RUSI), and the RAND Corporation–have also established offices in Qatar. During the initial diplomatic crisis of 2014, the governments

---

(163) Author's personal interviews, 1998 - 2002.

Chapter 6: The Evolution of Qatar's Education System

that started the crisis with Qatar targeted their rhetoric at both the Brookings Doha Centre and the RAND-Qatar Policy Institute, accusing them of conspiracy, sabotage, tampering, and corrupting minds. They demanded the closing of these institutions, which Qatar refused.

The Saudi leadership never implemented a blockade of Qatar during the 2014 crisis. However, at the onset of the blockade imposed by Saudi Arabia, Bahrain, and the UAE (together with Egypt) in June 2017, those countries issued a 13-point ultimatum that included the demand that "[Qatar must] align itself with the other Gulf and Arab countries militarily, politically, socially and economically."[164] To twist the knife further, the three Arabian Gulf blockading states ordered their citizens to leave Qatar within 15 days, leaving many Saudi and Emirati students unable to finish their university exams or complete their degrees.

For the western academic institutions that comprised Education City, the political environment of the early 2000s presented major risks. Gerd Nonneman, professor of International Relations and Gulf Studies at Georgetown University's School of Foreign Service in Qatar, and its dean from 2011 to 2016, recalled that when the Qataris first proposed the idea to Georgetown University in Washington, DC, "there was a lot of doubt." As Nonneman explained, "There was no financial risk"—in fact, the opportunity was a lucrative one for the school—but the "brand risk" was huge: if the proposal was instituted, a Jesuit Catholic institution would establish a satellite campus in a conservative Muslim country within a region known in the West for religious intolerance. However, in hindsight, these doubts proved overblown; the experiment has largely proved successful, and Georgetown did not experience any significant negative backlash in the United States.

Ultimately, Education City can best be described as an ambitious experiment with valuable lessons for both the American higher education system and those of emerging countries worldwide. Few countries have the deep pockets and relatively small population that gave Qatar the means to spend lavishly, offering foreign faculty

---

(164) Wintour, 2017.

the opportunity to work at high salaries at the branch campuses of top universities while granting generous scholarships to diverse students from countries worldwide.

Education City exemplifies Qatar's ability to break away from the ossification of Middle East politics, where regimes have historically imprisoned dissidents, journalists, activists, and academics. In contrast, Education City branches have highlighted the country's capability to widen boundaries and open up space for academics and students to express themselves more freely.

For example, academics at Georgetown University's School of Foreign Service in Qatar have researched the shortcomings in labor rights conditions in the country. In a more authoritarian environment, their research would have been suppressed, and some students might even have been arrested. Instead, their work has been published, enabling them to witness their own research contribute to reforms implemented by Doha authorities. Georgetown's Center for International and Regional Studies in Qatar has not been afraid to host forums on controversial and sensitive issues, such as GCC-Iran relations and sectarianism in the Middle East. These forums have been open to the public and have included academics visiting from Iran and Israel. The resulting scholarship has contributed meaningfully to learning throughout the Gulf and the Arab world.

The Education City project has not been cheap for Qatar. In 2016, the Washington Post reported that QF's annual budget for Education City exceeded $400 million. However, Qatari leaders believe that the investment is worth its cost, as it gives Qatar a leg up on achieving the "knowledge economy" so necessary for future competitiveness.[165]

While Education City has brought in many Western institutions, some experts contend that the presence of foreign universities detracts from the growth of local ones. As Ulrichsen noted, the growth of Education City "arguably occurred at the expense of [the] state-run Qatar University."[166] Looking to the future, one of the major challenges for Qatar in the sector of higher

---
(165) Attwood, 2016.
(166) Ulrichsen, 2016.

education will be to integrate its foreign universities with Qatari institutions in ways that can help the two further complement each other.

One example of such collaboration is the establishment in 2010 of Hamad bin Khalifa University (HBKU). Based at Education City, HBKU admitted its first students in 2014 and currently offers graduate degree programs in Law and Public Policy, Health and Life Sciences, Science and Engineering, Islamic Studies, and Humanities and Social Sciences. HBKU is expanding rapidly and is leaving a distinctly Qatari imprint on the Education City campus—as evidenced by the twin minarets on its Faculty of Islamic Studies building.

6.5. Enhancing the Qatar-U.S. Education Partnership

Qatari-American partnerships in the education sector witnessed important steps to enhance cooperation, some of which were signed during the strategic dialogue between the two countries in January 2019. Deputy Prime Minister and Minister of Foreign Affairs Sheikh Mohammed bin Abdul Rahman Al Thani and U.S. Secretary of State Mike Pompeo signed a memorandum of understanding in the field of education to continue building and sustaining key partnerships. Areas of cooperation include primary, secondary, and higher education, teaching English and Arabic, encouraging academic exchange, and providing a wide range of study options abroad to enable students to achieve their personal and professional goals.

The two governments stressed the importance of cooperation in the fields of education and culture. The dialogue discussed those subjects and signed a memorandum of understanding in the field. The two countries expressed the importance of continued cooperation in these areas and agreed to continue to work through the Bureau of Education and Culture of the U.S. Department of State. The United States also commended Qatar Foundation and its affiliated entities for their important work in the field of educational, research, and cultural programs jointly with leading American institutions in Doha, both through scholarships and with students who went on their own. By 2019, approximately 1,200 Qataris were studying in America.

The American universities in Education City graduate only a small fraction of Qataris; most of the students are third-country nationals, including a few U.S. citizens. However, the percentage of Qataris graduating from American institutions of higher learning has overtaken the number graduating from European (mostly British) schools and will certainly leave its imprint on the relationship.

The educational relationship between Qatar and the United States in the field of academic research and specialized education now produces high-quality graduates able to deal with the challenges of the times and the requirements of the labor market. Education City embodies a modern vision that foreshadows the promising future's foundations of culture, modern education, careful training, research, and smart opportunities that have provided a new generation of Qataris and the world with extensive knowledge.

It is important to emphasize the vital role played by the exceptional vision of Qatar's leadership in attracting the attention of American universities and pushing them to open branches in Education City. That vision was not the only reason that American universities decided to open branches in Qatar. Some of the universities decided to come to Qatar because of their desire to communicate and maintain a presence in the Middle East. After researching local conditions, these universities concluded that Qatar was the best place to undertake this engagement.

The Qatar-U.S. partnership has also helped in supporting and facilitating educational and cultural exchange programs that are under the supervision of the U.S. Embassy in Doha. These programs include study in the United States, the Fulbright program, the International Leadership for Visitors program, and specialized English language teaching programs, among many others.

6.6. Conclusion

The education process in Qatar over the past decades has witnessed many milestones and great challenges; Qatar has been successful in dealing with these challenges in a committed and responsible manner, moving from a traditional educational system, to building modern schools and universities, to the inauguration of the pioneering Education City complex.

Chapter 6: The Evolution of Qatar's Education System

The Education City project was established through the use of Qatari, American, and international expertise. Educational and scientific initiatives launched under the umbrella of the Qatar Foundation have become a critical component of the country's national vision to achieve its aspirations. Promoting higher education initiatives and producing graduates with strong qualifications are key to Qatar's future, as the country moves closer to the post-hydrocarbon period and aims to diversify its economy. Qatar's educational projects and initiatives have helped its citizens accomplish many significant achievements related to health, education, the arts, and other fields.

As one Gulf Times article in 2018 explained:

"The country's success in addressing the many challenges and difficult circumstances it has faced recently [...] has not been coincidental. Without a sound, correct foundation for advanced and modern education, in which Qatar invested in the past decade, the Qatari society would not have been able to overcome its difficulties."[167]

In sum, Qatar's distinguished multi-decade experience in the education system and local and international research partnerships has helped to strengthen the nation's soft power and supported its presence in regional and international forums.

---

(167) Gulf Times, 2018.

Photography

Qatari classroom, 1960s.

Qatari students, 1970s.

The layout of newly opened Qatar University, 1977.

The current campus of Qatar University.

Qatar's Education City campus.

Qatar National Library, 2020.

Photography

Georgetown University in Qatar.

Texas A&M University in Qatar.

Weill Cornell Medical College in Qatar.

Sheikha Moza meeting Secretary of State Hillary Clinton, 2009.

The VCU-Qatar Class of 2015.

Chapter 7
Qatar Becomes a Leader in International Media

7.1. Introduction

Unlike in the United States and much of the Western world, media institutions in Qatar are quite young. The first printed newspaper appeared in the middle of the twentieth century. Since then, Qatar's media industry has grown to worldwide stature, particularly the Al-Jazeera network, Qatar's flagship satellite channel. Since its launch in 1996, it has become an international competitor and partner to many American media giants. In a way, Al Jazeera is one of the worldwide satellite news channels that followed the appearance of CNN. Over the past 25 years, Al Jazeera has radically changed the media landscape in the Middle East and played a key role in the twenty-first century's major political milestones.

7.2. The Media Landscape in Qatar

The emergence of visual, audio, and print media in the Gulf states in general (and Qatar in particular) trailed not only the West but also many other Arab countries. Small populations, weak formal education, widespread illiteracy, and low penetration of standardized Arabic inhibited the growth and spread of mass media. In addition, economic factors, such as the early twentieth-century depression in the Gulf economies caused by the collapse of the pearl trade, discouraged investment in mass media. While Britain, the region's former colonial power, tolerated the existence of newspapers and magazines, it had little interest in the emergence of local media in the Gulf States it "protected."[168]

---

(168) Al-Jaber and Gunter, 2013.

Chapter 7: Qatar Becomes a Leader in International Media

Print media predated audiovisual media in Qatar and the Gulf. A number of daily and weekly newspapers, as well as literary and cultural magazines, began publication in the late 1950s and early 1960s. While it drew on the experience of media in other Arab countries, the Qatari media community has forged its own path to address the specific conditions that led to development in Qatar in the last decades.

Not surprisingly, political events ranging from the World Wars, the Cold War, the Arab-Israeli conflict, the Iranian Revolution, the Iran-Iraq War, and the establishment of the Gulf Cooperation Council (GCC) impacted the development of Qatar's media. Regional and international political trends and events provided the fodder for the growth of media outlets and the formulation of the perceptions of the small Gulf country.

Historically, Qatar has been involved in printing and publishing books since the advent of printing in the surrounding region. The founder of modern Qatar, Sheikh Jassim, authored and published one of the first books in the Gulf Arab countries when he ordered the printing of his book Risala Bush'r Al-Nabati (Message in Traditional Poetry) from the Mustafawiyya Press in Mumbai, India, in 1907. This poetry diwan (collection) of Sheikh Jassim became an important reference for the study of the historical and social conditions of Qatar and the Gulf in the early twentieth century, as well as a record of important events in the region during the previous four centuries. It also included poems written by the Sheikh and other contemporary poets in that period of time and before.[169]

Credit goes to Abdulla Hussain Na'ama, the first Dean of the Qatari press, for establishing the first printing press in Qatar in 1955.[170] With the oil boom and its accompanying increase in revenue, the tiny emirate quickly attracted leading journalistic and cultural talent from the more developed press sectors of the Arab region and the larger world.

---

(169) Al-Rumaihi, 2012.
(170) Ibid.

7.3. Qatari Print Media

Print media began in Qatar with the establishment of an oil company newsletter in 1960, followed by the publication of the official government gazette Al Jareeda Al-Rasmiyah in 1961. Qatar later established the Department of Information in 1969, which released Majallat Al-Doha (Doha Magazine) in the same year. Moreover, the Ministry of Education began issuing Majallat Al-Tarbiya (Education Magazine) one year later. In 1979, Sahifat Al-Urooba (Pan-Arabism Press) and Gulf News (a bimonthly English-language magazine) were launched as the first private press publications in Qatar.[171]

Qatar's first private daily newspaper, Al-Arab, printed its first edition in 1972. The current daily newspapers are among the oldest publications in Qatar, including Al-Raya, Al-Sharq, and Al-Watan, all of which began printing in the 1970s. The oldest of the three is Al-Raya, from May 1979, followed by Al-Sharq with its first issue in 1986 and Al-Watan in September 1995.

In addition to Arabic newspapers, Al-Raya Press also launched the first private English-speaking newspaper, the Gulf Times, in December 1978. Al-Sharq followed with its English edition, The Peninsula, in 1996. Finally, Al-Watan Press's English-language publication the Qatar Tribune published its first issue in September 2006. In addition to these broadsheets, Qatar boasts many other publications covering politics, business, society, finance, health, art, and entertainment.

The Qatari government began providing financial support to local newspapers and presses upon the establishment of the Ministry of Information in 1979. However, it stopped this practice in 1995 when Qatar abolished the Ministry of Information—making it the only country in the Arab world at that time without a censoring body—and delegated its responsibilities to various independent bodies, including a National Council for Culture, Arts and Heritage and a Radio and Television Authority.

---

(171) Ismail, 2004

Chapter 7: Qatar Becomes a Leader in International Media

This left the press and other domestic media essentially free from direct government interference and censorship. It also allowed many national and international newspapers and magazines to appear on the Qatari market, such as the New York Times, the Washington Post, Time, Financial Times, and Al Quds Alarabi.[172]

7.4. Radio Broadcasting

The first radio broadcasts in Qatar began in 1968. The pioneer in this field was Mosque Radio, which broadcast sermons and reached audiences in the Doha area. In June 1968, Qatar Radio acquired Mosque Radio's transmission facilities. The Qatar Broadcasting Service (QBS) began airing radio programming in Arabic, adding English, Urdu, and French programming to the lineup in 1971, 1980, and 1985 respectively. Moreover, international radio stations, such as the BBC, Voice of America, and Radio Sawa (the last two funded by the U.S. government), have also been made available.[173]

A new entry into the radio sector that has spread widely in Qatar and the Gulf states is the Voice of the Gulf Radio, launched by the Qatar Media Foundation in 2002, aimed at documenting and highlighting Gulf Arab heritage. The station has broadcast thousands of unique songs from over 70 artists and poets from the Gulf, Arabian Peninsula, and around the world. The Voice of the Gulf hosts the annual Doha Music Festival and in addition to its arts programming, broadcasts local and regional sporting competitions.

7.5. Television Broadcasting

Qatar Television began broadcasting in 1970. Its early black-and-white programming broadcast only during afternoons from 3:00 pm to 7:00 pm. With the advent of color television in 1974, transmission was extended to nine hours per day. This pattern continued to develop until 1982 when Channel 2 in English was launched to broadcast cultural programs, sporting events, and other special programs.[174]

Among the initiatives that supported the TV production sector was the launch of Al Rayyan Media and Marketing Company, which also operates Al Rayyan Satellite Channel, established on

---

(172) Al-Jaber et. al., 2005.
(173) Al-Jaber et. al., 2003.
(174) Al-Zayani and Ayesh, 2006.

May 23, 2012. The channel focuses on addressing Qatari society as a primary audience and has developed programming and content aimed at Qatari national identity and aspirations. It designed its vision and programming strategy to support the Qatar National Vision 2030, with the goal of achieving sustainable development through three main functions: development, awareness, and entertainment.

7.6. Digital Media

The internet arrived in the Arab world late, but it has boomed over the past two decades. Internet usage in the Arab world grew significantly from 2000 to 2007, in conjunction with the release of the second generation of the internet. In recent years, online media has greatly influenced the global communication scene; digital media platforms have fundamentally shifted how content and various activities and tasks are executed.

Qatar has not fallen behind. Internet usage in Qatar has grown significantly; according to one study, it jumped from 85 percent in 2013 to 95 percent by 2018.[175] That study looked at internet usage in Qatar by age groups, finding that Qataris between the ages of 25 and 34 had close to 100 percent usage, and 96 percent of those aged from 18 to 24 years used the internet regularly. The age group from 35 to 44 reported 97 percent utilization, while usage among those over 45 years old decreased to 82 percent.

The study found that the consumption of traditional media (television, radio, newspapers, and magazines) registered a significant decline of 15 percent among Qataris, from 87 percent in 2013 to 72 percent in 2017. Print publications have seen a 34 percent decline in readership over the last five years. Only 29 percent of Qataris in 2017 indicated that they still read print newspapers and magazines, compared to 67 percent in 2013. Reading of magazines further decreased from 22 percent in 2013 to only 9 percent in 2017.

A study published in 2017 by Northwestern University in Qatar revealed that Qataris are extremely connected to digital media.[176] The Northwestern study indicated that nearly 100 percent of Qataris use the internet and spend about 60 percent more time on

---
(175) Dennis et. al., 2017.
(176) Al-Jaber & Elareshi, 2016.

Chapter 7: Qatar Becomes a Leader in International Media

the web than citizens of other regional countries. The study showed that Qatar has unique patterns in its usage of social media; some 93 percent of Qataris use WhatsApp, while 70 percent use Instagram and 64 percent use Snapchat—two of the highest utilization rates in the world. Qataris spent about 44.5 hours per week on the internet in 2017, compared with 36.9 hours in 2013, the highest in the region.[177]

Social media plays a powerful role in Qatar. Social media platforms are considered open spheres that allow Qatari citizens to express their views on politics, society, religion, and other delicate issues that were formerly taboo. This has influenced political, social, and religious speech in most Gulf countries including Qatar. Social media has also enabled sectors previously marginalized by traditional Gulf societies, such as young people and women, to engage with their politicians, religious leaders, intellectuals, and other elites.[178] Social media provides a platform to address grievances and pro-mote a more equal society.[179]

Unlike traditional media, social media platforms offer a more effective space for discussion and debate. Social media has changed the rules of dialogue, democratized public spaces, and introduced inexperienced players to the world of political communication. The intellectual influence of new media activists in society has far surpassed the influence of the old traditional intellectual elite. Moreover, the citizens of these countries have grown used to presenting their ideas outside of traditional media, making political demands, and breaking social taboos. In Qatar, for example, social media has opened discussions on issues such as democracy, political and economic changes, feminism, foreign workers in Qatar, and government corruption.[180]

---

(177) Al-Jaber & Elareshi, 2016.
(178) Ahmed, 2016.
(179) Al-Jaber & Elareshi, 2016.
(180) Linaker, 2014.

7.7. Reaching Regional and International Audiences

In the late 1980s and early 1990s, the introduction of the satellite dish to the Middle East changed the region's news and media landscape in unprecedented ways. Prior to the introduction of satellite television, all sources of news—print media, radio, and traditional TV broadcasting—were physically controlled by the government and subject to censorship. In one notorious case, following Iraq's August 1990 invasion of Kuwait, the Saudi government declined to tell any of its citizens for several days, to prevent a panic and allow them time to formulate a strategy.

The advent of satellite television—which could be broadcast from New York or London and picked up in Cairo or Baghdad via satellite dish, and was (at first) virtually impossible for local governments to censor—destroyed the ability of governments to control what their people saw or heard. After some initial and unsuccessful attempts to ban satellite dishes, most Arab regimes relented, and the floodgates of information were irrevocably opened. The Gulf War displayed the potential for satellite television: it was sometimes described as the "video game war" in the West for its unprecedented coverage. The American network CNN, in particular, was distinguished for its comprehensive and up-to-date reporting, which was widely viewed throughout the Middle East and directly inspired the creation of the Al-Jazeera network five years later. Al Jazeera, the largest and most controversial Arabic news channel, is a phenomenon that one can only comprehend if one understands the special conditions of the region out of which it arose. The tremors caused by the Iraqi invasion of Kuwait, the consequences of the 9/11 attacks, and the U.S.-led invasion of Iraq in 2003 resulted in extreme social and political chaos and disorder throughout the region.

Al Jazeera played a prominent role in closely and constantly covering these unprecedented events and changes in the region. The channel has been distinguished from other state-owned TV stations by its comprehensive, around-the-clock coverage and its focus on fairness and presenting all sides of a story.

Chapter 7: Qatar Becomes a Leader in International Media

On March 23, 2006, Al Jazeera officially became a network when it combined its main channel to Al Jazeera Live, Al Jazeera Sports, Al Jazeera English, Al Jazeera Documentary Channel, Al Jazeera for Children, Al Jazeera Net Training and Development Center, and Al Jazeera Studies Center.[181]

7.8. Al Jazeera's Popularity and Uniqueness

Al Jazeera's popularity rose as that of other Arab media declined. One anecdote reports that by the late 1990s, almost every Arab leader across the region with a TV in their office had it permanently tuned to Al Jazeera.[182]

Al Jazeera Network built a reputation of fierce independence, professionalism, objectivity, and focus on the issues that mattered most to Arab publics. For decades, the Arab people as a whole had no confidence in government-controlled national media. Almost all Middle Eastern countries have a cabinet ministry managing the flow of information and censoring all media outlets. These "Ministries of Information" are generally regarded as vehicles for censorship and state-run media as propaganda designed to support a national political agenda rather than to tell the truth.

In contrast, Al Jazeera quickly grabbed the attention of the Arab world by its objective coverage of the 2000 Palestinian Intifada and the American invasions and occupations of Afghanistan and Iraq. These broadcasts energized freedom of expression and Arab public discussion on previously taboo topics such as political freedom, democracy, human rights, criticism of the ruling authority, Arab relations with the U.S. and Israel, and the passivity of most Arab states regarding the Palestinian conflict. Mark Lynch, a professor of political science and international affairs at George Washington University, noted that by the time the Arab Spring protests erupted in 2011, Al Jazeera was already the preferred station of both Arab and Western viewers and was "the unquestioned home of the revolution on the airwaves."[183] Al Jazeera's journalists have repeatedly "scooped" their competitors around the world. They have also changed the face of reporting from conflict, unveiling the

---

(181) Dennis et. al., 2017.
(182) Ibid.
(183) Lynch, 2014.

Chapter 7: Qatar Becomes a Leader in International Media

real human cost of war and broadcasting scenes of destruction and images of civilian casualties.[184]

This makes Al Jazeera unique and a quantum leap forward in the development of Arab media. Until the arrival of Al Jazeera, if Arab viewers wanted uncensored news, they had to rely on international news agencies and Western satellite TV stations that presented issues only from a Western perspective. Al Jazeera was also the first Arab channel to introduce proper investigative journalism and the first to entertain guests with differing opinions on its talk shows, dramatically expanding the boundaries of free speech and tackling previously forbidden topics. For the first time, Arab viewers saw programs devoted to discussing subjects such as suicide bombing and the existence of God. Al Jazeera broke social, political, and religious taboos and deployed a network of correspondents who brought current affairs to Arab viewers live.

When it was launched, Al Jazeera's new standards of reporting and its uncensored programs caused a major disruption to the Arab world.[185] From its first broadcasts, Al Jazeera grabbed the attention of opinion-makers, academics, and politicians across the political spectrum, as well as the general public.[186] Egyptian President Hosni Mubarak marveled at the network's small office and production staff when he visited Al Jazeera's building in Qatar: "All the tempest comes out from this matchbox?" His surprise may have reflected chagrin that Qatar had supplanted Egypt as the Mecca of Arab media, despite Egyptian state media's vast advantages in money, manpower, and technology.[187]

For the first time, Al Jazeera's coverage of the 2001 invasion of Afghanistan led Western media to quote Arab media sources. In the first two weeks of the American-led invasion in October 2001, Al Jazeera was the only international satellite TV outlet broadcasting from Kabul; CNN and other major satellite channels simply rebroadcast footage from Al Jazeera teams for the first week of the invasion. Al Jazeera's experience in rising to the level of "best of foreign broadcasting" provided a successful model for the Arab satellite TV stations that followed.[188]

---

(184) Henderson, 2001.
(185) Campagna, 2001.
(186) Auter et. al., 2004.
(187) Auter et. al., 2004.
(188) El-Nawawy and Iskandar, 2002.

Chapter 7: Qatar Becomes a Leader in International Media

The Al Jazeera phenomenon has created controversy in the Arab world. Some see it as a positive disruption of the stagnant Arab media narrative, generating a welcome wave of differing opinions. Others, generally those with a conservative perspective, accuse the network of driving wedges between Arabs rather than enlightening them. Al Jazeera has received criticism from virtually every Arab newspaper, television and radio station, internet site, and the majority of Arab, Middle Eastern, and Western governments.[189]

Based on Al Jazeera's willingness to give time to leaders and policymakers from different backgrounds, it has been repeatedly accused of sympathy for those factions. When Al Jazeera interviewed then Iraqi president Saddam Hussein, critics accused it of being a mouthpiece of the Iraqi regime. Its interview with Israeli Minister of Foreign Affairs Shimon Peres led to the accusation that it gave a platform to Israeli leaders and served the interests of the Israeli enemy. Its broadcast of Iranian celebrations and interviews of former Secretary of State Madeleine Albright provoked negative commentary from the United States and Iran. Giving airtime to the Taliban Government's Ambassador in Islamabad led to Al Jazeera being labeled pro-Taliban.[190] Broadcasting Osama Bin Laden's statements provoked American anger, while its broadcasts of American leaders attacking Osama bin Laden and Al-Qaeda led to accusations that Al Jazeera was reinforcing an American campaign blaming Islam for the 9/11 attacks.

Al Jazeera's bold media approach has also caused political complications for Qatar, angering both Arab states and U.S. administrations at different times. Some countries threatened to sever diplomatic relations, while others closed down Al Jazeera's offices and expelled or jailed their correspondents. Notably, closing Al Jazeera has been an ongoing demand by other Arab countries since 2003 and was one of the fourteen demands imposed on Qatar during the 2017-2021 Gulf diplomatic crisis.

---

(189) Koranteng, 1999.
(190) Rugh, 2004.

7.9. Al Jazeera English and the United States

Al Jazeera has two principal news channels: Al Jazeera Arabic (AJA) and Al Jazeera English (AJE). AJE differs from AJA in terms of language, content, programs, priorities, and frame of reference. This should not come as a surprise, as they serve different audiences.

Foreign (non-Arab) audiences have grown familiar with AJE, which has a sophisticated news program and wide distribution. Most observers regard AJE as comparable to English language international news channels, such as BBC World, CNN International, and France24. Al Jazeera English went live in 2006 with lofty editorial aims. Journalism professor William Youmans of George Washington University writes in An Unlikely Audience, his history of Al Jazeera's expansion to English, that the ambition was to "cover parts of the world to which the global news titans gave scant attention: Southwest Asia, Sub-Saharan Africa, Latin America, and urban ghettos in the West." Its news agenda would range from "poverty and the plight of minority groups, to the social, cultural, and environmental costs of global capitalism and power politics."

This strategy earned AJE little attention until the 2011 Arab Spring, when revolutions broke out in Tunisia, Egypt, Libya, and Yemen. During the Arab Spring, AJE became the international go-to channel for coverage of the Arab protests. Although its coverage was sometimes controversial, its live-streaming attracted over 1.6 million American viewers to its website. This solidified the network's reputation in the United States, and the station's management decided to pursue an ambitious expansion into the U.S. market.

The network's comprehensive coverage also gained it support from various corners, typically from those aligned with the goals of the Arab Spring. Former Secretary of State Hillary Clinton testified before the U.S. Senate on March 2, 2011, opining that Al Jazeera's U.S. prominence was growing because it offered "real news." Speaking before the Senate Foreign Relations Committee, Clinton said the United States was losing the world's "information war"; other countries' global news outlets, she said, were making more inroads into places like the Middle East than American media. She

Chapter 7: Qatar Becomes a Leader in International Media

cited the quality of channels like Al Jazeera as an example, claiming that it was "changing peoples' minds and attitudes. And like it or hate it, it is really effective." U.S. news, she added, was not keeping up.[191]

Due to its significant success in attracting American viewers, in August 2013, Al Jazeera Media Network launched Al Jazeera America (AJAM), an American cable news channel. It made inroads after its parent company paid former Vice President Al Gore and his partners $500 million for Current TV, a small cable channel.

AJAM was conceived as a sister channel to AJE, Al Jazeera's international English language news channel. Although the two operated separately, they shared studios and bureaus. AJAM also ran some of AJE's programming but created most of its live newscasts and programs on its own. However, the network ultimately failed, despite AJAM's building of a loyal U.S. audience and its reputation as an important new voice in television news. The network did not gain sufficient advertisement traction and financial revenues and shut down in 2016. Although AJAM's closure was not a positive development for the station, it weakens the argument that Al Jazeera serves as an extension of Qatar's foreign policy. The fact that AJAM failed to compete in the news market suggests instead that, rather than a state-funded propaganda outlet, it is a media institution like any other, subject to the same pressures and obligations as any Western channel.

Although AJAM's journey came to an end, Al Jazeera English, which has U.S. bureaus in Washington, New York, Chicago, Miami, and Los Angeles, continues its success and is now being carried in the U.S. as a live stream on digital platforms. Its English-language reports have won international awards, including Peabody and International Emmy Awards.

Nonetheless, political opposition to the channel continues. In June 2019, six U.S. senators and two representatives sent a letter requesting that the Department of Justice (DOJ) review whether the net-work ought to register as a foreign agent. The letter argued that "Al Jazeera is a messaging tool for the Qatari government"

---

(191) Folkenflik, 2011.

and request-ed that the DOJ demand that AJC register under the Foreign Agents Registration Act.[192] Another such letter was sent to the DOJ in 2020.

In a statement to the Washington Examiner, the network responded, asserting that Al Jazeera "is not owned by Qatar" and that "its reporting is not directed or controlled by the Qatari government, nor does it reflect any government viewpoint." Moreover, the request may have been prompted by Gulf politics. According to Bloomberg, the United Arab Emirates—politically opposed to Qatar and one of the countries involved in the 2017-2021 blockade—ran a lobbying campaign in the United States in an attempt to delegitimize Al Jazeera. Per the report, the UAE also mounted a separate digital information operation involving UAE-controlled Twitter accounts and websites hiding their affiliations.[193]

Despite this negative campaign in the United States, the network continued to broaden its reach by adapting new technology. In 2014, the channel launched Al Jazeera Plus (AJ+), a U.S.-based online news channel. By May 2019, AJ+ had 11.1 million cumulative followers and subscribers on Facebook and was ranked fortieth as an "overall creator" of content cross-platform.

Ultimately bowing to political pressure, the U.S. forced AJ+ to register as an "agent of a foreign government." CNN reported that the order came on the eve of the signing ceremony of the Abraham Accords between Israel and two of Qatar's bitter Gulf rivals, Bahrain and the UAE. CNN also reported speculation that the two Gulf governments demanded this U.S. action as a price for signing the Accords with Israel.[194]

---

(192) Bandler, 2019.
(193) Light, 2019.
(194) Atwood, 2020.

Chapter 7: Qatar Becomes a Leader in International Media

7.10. Conclusion

Qatar's media jumped from the first printing press in the mid-1950s to a position of leadership in Arab, regional, and international media in less than 70 years. The peninsula's media outlets have created the opportunity for unprecedented public debate in the Arab world and outreach across the globe.

In 2019, the Qatari Council of Ministers approved the establishment of Media City, a hub for regional media outlets in Doha. The Qatar Media City project aims to enhance the role of local media while also attracting international media outlets. Media City provides incentives to attract investment, such as exemptions from taxes and customs, as well as providing an attractive environment for international media. Although it is a free zone, the laws of the state will apply to all institutions in the city; but since those laws expressly protect freedom of the press, this caveat offers no barriers to Media City's development.[195]

As in many other countries, new media outlets and social media in Qatar have fundamentally changed the landscape. Cell phones play an enormous role in this transition, as many Qataris link their social media usage to the accessibility of hand-held devices. As a result, traditional media consumption in Qatar has significantly declined. WhatsApp and Snapchat are among the most widely used social media platforms among Qataris, and the internet penetration rate in Qatar is among the highest worldwide.

In Qatar, new media also offers a broad range of ideas based on expression, dialogue, open discussion, and the dissemination of news and information. This can be termed "communication democracy," as it involves widespread participation by the vast majority of people, particularly marginalized segments of society, such as women and young people, who represent the majority and the future of the GCC region. Although many obstacles and challenges have hindered Qatar's efforts to encourage the optimal use of these newcommunication platforms and applications, they have been acknowledged and are being addressed.

---

(195) QNA, 2019.

In short, with its media-friendly atmosphere, Qatar remains almost unique in the region, with a landscape that contrasts with the government-controlled local television stations, radio stations, and newspapers that have typified long-standing repressive and authoritarian regimes throughout the greater Arab world.

Photography

Al Jazeera Arabic headquarters in Doha.

Al Jazeera English headquarters in Doha.

Al Jazeera's Washington, DC bureau office.

Al Jazeera America, which closed in 2016.

"The Opposite Direction," one of the most popular shows on Al Jazeera.

BeIn Sports, the dominant sports network in the Middle East.

Photography

Qatari daily press.

Qatar TV channel.

Al Rayyan TV channel.

A Qatari radio station.

A media survey conducted by Northwestern University in Qatar.

Qatar Media Corporation headquarters.

Chapter 8
Doha's Soft Power: Culture, Art, and Museums

8.1. Introduction

It is no surprise that the cultural and artistic scene in the United States and other Western countries differs greatly from that of the capitals of the Arab world. The instability and violence of the last few decades battered the traditional cultural centers of the Middle East in Baghdad, Cairo, Beirut, and Damascus. The American-led invasion of Iraq in 2003, the Arab Spring uprisings of 2011, and the subsequent full-scale civil war in Syria drove the locus of culture and academia elsewhere in the region. In particular, Arab artists and intellectuals have gravitated toward the Arabian Gulf where they have found that the GCC states provide a relatively safe haven to innovate. Moreover, in addition to the relative tranquility and security of the GCC states, their wealth provides a powerful incentive to migrate to Doha and other Arabian Peninsula cities.

Qatar is considered one of the main centers for attracting artists and innovators in the Arab world. It is a maritime country with a long history of tolerance and welcoming strangers from all over the world, and it has demonstrated a particular attraction for the world of art and culture. This reputation has been burnished by the Qatari government's heavy investments in cultural projects, events, international conferences, and museums as part of its efforts to make the country an important cultural center both in and beyond the Arab and Islamic worlds.

Chapter 8: Doha's Soft Power: Culture, Art and Museums

Blending local, Arab, and Islamic traditions with modernity has enhanced Qatar's role as a modern-day Middle Eastern hub for art. Qatar's interest in human heritage has led it to build numerous museums whose curators have been given the freedom to procure important and relevant art from a diverse group of countries. These museums also help the Qatari people share their perspectives, stories, and culture with visitors from around the globe. Qatar's cultural program has created vibrant art and cultural scene in Doha that has won international praise and put Qatar on the cultural map of the world.

8.2. Doha's Cultural Landscape

In Qatar, the old traditions and architecture of the Arabian Desert exists side-by-side with the trappings of modernity: skyscrapers, expensive restaurants, and luxury cars. Qatar's expanding labor market attracts not only construction laborers but also hundreds of thousands of educated and highly skilled professionals who expect a high standard of living. Altogether, Qatar is a fascinating cultural mosaic, and it is home to the second-largest expatriate community in the world. Qatar's booming economy has allowed the country to invest in culture, including world-renowned museums, art galleries, film festivals, and open-air concerts. At the same time, the country has never ignored its historical traditions, and it presents itself today as a forward-thinking, modern society that maintains a deep connection to its past.

The Qatari people are descendants of both nomadic Bedouin tribes and the settled maritime communities of the Gulf. This background has created a vibrant blend of culture, one associated with the nation's past and full of the legacy of the Arab and Islamic civilization that developed and blended with other cultures in the region for many centuries.

Qatar's official language is Arabic, but the country has integrated many foreign languages, especially English, into its social, economic, and educational activities. In the process, it has not ignored the many other languages spoken by its diverse expatriate community, not least among them Farsi and the many languages of the Indian subcontinent.

Although the world sees the expatriate community as a late twentieth-century phenomenon and a product of the oil boom, Qatar's many centuries of trade and contact with multiple societies of the Gulf and the Indian Ocean have left a cultural imprint on the country's traditions.

While nearly all Qataris identify as Muslim and Qatari society tends toward conservatism in many aspects, both government and society display acceptance and tolerance of other religious identities. The law imposes no restrictions on other faiths and protects them against attack and criticism.

8.3. Qatari Society

Qatari society is heavily influenced by Islamic customs, and the dress code is generally traditional and conservative. Both women and men wear the national dress. Qatari Arab men usually wear a flowing white full-length robe (thawb) over trousers and an undershirt with sandals and a keffiyeh (a white headscarf draped over the head) held on with an agal (a black rope). Qatari Arab women wear a full-length black dress (abaya), generally over Western clothing, and many also wear the veil (hijab).

Qatari written literature developed only recently, with the modern literature movement beginning in the late twentieth century. An oral tradition of poetry has been popular in Qatar since pre-Islamic times. Poetry passed on age-old traditions, beliefs, and folktales through many generations. The prosperity generated by the discovery of oil in the twentieth century brought with it, among other positive developments, a dramatic increase in the levels of education and literacy, ushering in a literary revolution. Today, Qatar's literacy rate approaches 100 percent, and both female and male writers have contributed extensively to Qatari literature.

Qatar's folk music is closely associated with the sea, and many folk songs are based on pearl diving. A popular Qatari folk dance is known as the Ardah, in which two rows of men (sometimes carrying swords) face each other and dance to the music of drums and spoken poetry.[196] Songs sung by women are generally related to

---

(196) Sen Nag, 2018.

their daily activities. Women would also sing about the hardships of pearl diving when greeting the pearl ships returning to harbor.[197]

8.4. Katara (Cultural Village Foundation)

The Cultural Village Foundation (Katara) is one of the most important and prominent cultural institutions in the country. It is located on the shores of the sea between the West Bay and The Pearl on the eastern coast of Qatar. Its buildings take inspiration from traditional Gulf architecture, which spread in the Gulf region during the pearl-diving era before the discovery of oil. The paths and alleys of Katara were intentionally made to be narrow and winding, giving modern Qataris and visitors an understanding of a historical Arab city's layout. They lead the visitor to the cultural district. Within Katara, Shakespeare Street is the most famous destination.

Today, more than a decade after its 2010 inauguration, the Cultural Village is considered one of the most important landmarks on Qatar's tourism, entertainment, cultural, and heritage map. It is the largest modern cultural project in Qatar, and arguably also in the Gulf and the Middle East region at large. It is a place where the audience and the visitor meet to experience a gathering of different world cultures by attending daily events in the halls or on the beach, in addition to theaters, artistic performances, concerts, creative workshops, restaurants, cafes, and advanced capacities.[198]

Tracking Qatar through history provides a fascinating backdrop to the nation's current cultural and educational wealth. This cultural richness plays a very important role in promoting and building Qatari society. The attachment to Qatar's ancient roots, together with modernization and technological progress, form a solid foundation for its modern personality and values.

Small wonder, then, that there are so many artists, sculptors, and musicians present in the Cultural Village. Katara is a hub for Qatar's cultural venues, including its Greco-Roman amphitheater that seats five thousand. The theater has hosted a variety of cultural activities, from international music acts to folk dancers from around the world. For smaller-scale performances, there are drama theatres,

---
(197) Sen Nag, 2019.
(198) Katara, 2020.

an opera house (the residence of the Qatar Philharmonic Orchestra), film festivals, art exhibitions, poetry, jazz, and more. Katara Village also hosts the Qatar Fine Arts Society, the Visual Art Centre, the Childhood Cultural Centre, the Qatar Photographic Society, the Qatar Music Academy, and the Qatar Theatre Society.[199]

8.5. Souq Waqif

Souq Waqif is an important heritage market in Qatar, as well as a major tourism landmark. It ranks as one of the most famous traditional folk markets in the region and displays various traditional goods offered for sale to visitors.

According to Qatari historians, the souq dates back about 250 years and was called "Souq Waqif" because the sellers used to stand at the entrances to display their wares that included spices, cumin, cinnamon, fish, clothes, and wood. In Arabic, the word 'waqif' means 'standing' and 'souq' means 'market'—hence the name "Standing Market."

The traditional marketplace is located near the central area of the Doha Corniche and underwent an extensive renovation in the twenty-first century that transformed the area into a thriving heritage district. The renovated Souq Waqif combines elements both of the old—the warren of narrow streets and shops in the covered souq—with the new—boutiques and hotels that cater to residents and visitors alike who flock to the area. A marketplace has long existed at Souq Waqif, where Bedouin traders from the desert interior met with fishermen and traders whose boats imported goods from as far afield as India and the African coastline.

Much of Souq Waqif declined in the 1980s and 1990s, and in 2003 a fire destroyed most of what remained of the original market. The Qatari government, however, took on a project to rebuild the market and restore its traditional architecture. The renovation proved to be an enormous success, and Souq Waqif is today one of the most visited areas of Doha. Qatari citizens and residents continue to flock to Souq Waqif, appreciating the authenticity of the restoration. The restoration of Souq Waqif and the surrounding area is one of the most successful examples of urban redevelopment in the Gulf region.[200]

---

(199) The Telegraph, 2018
(200) BBC News, 2011..

Chapter 8: Doha's Soft Power: Culture, Art and Museums

Souq Waqif has also become a cultural and entertainment hub in Qatar, hosting many festivals. With the opening of Doha Metro, it is very easy to reach the Souq from any part of Qatar. Qatar Museum recently chose Souq Waqif as the site for Le Pouce, a public art installation, linking the historic heart of the city with a piece of modern history. Le Pouce, in the shape of a giant thumb, is one of its creator's best-known pieces and a popular example of his tendency to create larger-than-life experiences. Le Pouce is the latest addition to Qatar's extensive public art collection, which aims to connect audiences living in and visiting Qatar with inspiring works of art through unexpected interactions in daily life.[201]

8.6. Qatari Museums

Museums have become prominent features of all Gulf States, playing an important role in fostering and projecting a national identity. This process began to unfold during the 1960s and 1970s, as Qatar's newly gained independence fostered nation-building. Creating and curating a national story that described the transformation of tribal societies into modern states was especially important at a time of rapid socioeconomic modernization. As the nature of both the state and society changed beyond recognition within the time span of a single generation, the sense that these shifts were part of a broader and evolving national story was an integral part of the formulation of a national identity for Qatar, as it was for Qatar's neighbors.

In 1975, Qatar's national museum opened in the palace where Sheikh Abdullah bin Jassim Al Thani, ruler of Qatar from 1913 to 1949, lived for the decade following his accession. The museum displays archeological artifacts, tools, and implements from the era of Qatar's pearling industry. Half a century after the seat of Qatari power moved to the present-day location of the Amiri Diwan, Sheikh Abdullah's palace was revived as the Qatar National Museum. Opening only four years after Qatar gained its independence, the Qatar National Museum played a significant role in anchoring the rapid economic changes brought about by oil money in a greater awareness of the past.

Many of the objects in the museum's collection are sourced from European archaeologists whose excavations in the Arabian

---
(201) The Peninsula, 2020.

Chapter 8: Doha's Soft Power: Culture, Art and Museums

Gulf began in the 1950s. In 1973, Doha invited the renowned British archeologist Beatrice de Cardi, a fellow of the Society of Antiquaries of London, to lead an expedition to enrich Qatar's national story for the museum. The country commissioned De Cardi, who had first worked in Balochistan (Pakistan) in 1947, to collect material in order to "tell the story of Qatar from the start of the Neolithic (c. 6000–5000 BC) to the present day."[202] As The Guardian noted, "The day after [de Cardi's] retirement in 1973, she was in Qatar, commissioned by the government to uncover the country's story 'from the Stone Age to the Oil Age' in 10 weeks."[203]

The purpose of Qatar's national museum was twofold. First, the museum was "to construct a distinct national identity linked to the past," and second, "to preserve a changing lifestyle."[204] From the Qatari perspective, both elements were crucial for the newly independent country to distinguish itself from other Middle Eastern nations.

As scholars Karen Exell and Trinidad Rico wrote:

"The museum as the place of representation with its single authoritative narrative went unchallenged as a model of heritage representation in Qatar and the surrounding Gulf States. In retrospect, and forty years on, it seems that the museum effected a conceptual change on methods of presenting and validating local identity."[205]

Following Sheikh Hamad's ascent to power in June 1995, the Qatari government began placing greater emphasis on heritage development. The ambitious emir believed in Qatar's ability to present itself as "the heart of Islamic culture and to develop Qatar as a tourist destination."[206] The emir's wife, Sheikha Mozah, and his two daughters, Sheikha Al Mayassa and Sheikha Hind, played leading roles in the development of Doha as an arts and cultural capital.

Three years after Sheikh Hamad took the throne, the Supreme Council of Culture, Arts and Heritage was established. Next, the Qatar Tourist Authority and the Qatar Museums Authority were formed

---

(202) Exell and Rico, 2013.
(203) Pitts, 2016.
(204) Exell and Rico, 2013.
(205) Ibid.
(206) Ibid.

Chapter 8: Doha's Soft Power: Culture, Art and Museums

in 2000 and 2005. Over the first two decades of the twenty-first century, the building of new museums came to play a major role in the transformation of the Doha skyline, especially around the iconic Corniche, and branded Qatar as a regional hub of arts and culture.

Doha's museums help educate people around the globe about the Arabian Gulf country's heritage, as well as its future aspirations, which can only be understood within the context of Qatar's past. The Doha museums are therefore a key component in the emirate's soft power foreign policy agenda.

8.7. The Museum of Islamic Art

The Museum of Islamic Art rises on an artificial peninsula on the Corniche. Designed as a cubistic pyramid, this 45,000-square-meter museum is an iconic feature of the Qatari capital's skyline. The museum was designed by internationally-renowned architect I.M. Pei, who had previously designed the entrance to the Louvre museum in Paris; the museum was his final work of art.[207] At the age of 90, Pei traveled to numerous Arab and Islamic countries to take inspiration from their various Islamic buildings. Egypt's Ibn Tulun Mosque served as his main source of inspiration.[208] As Pei explained, the Ibn Tulun Mosque "is very austere and beautiful, and features the most refined geometry" and what "inspired [him] the most was the small ablution fountain in the middle of a large courtyard. That little building is a poem".[209]

Emir Sheikh Hamad presided over the opening of the museum in November 2018, and it immediately became a signature, and instantly recognizable, feature of the cityscape. The Wall Street Journal described the museum as a "staggered set of creamy building blocks, each cube adjusted just enough to catch a triangle of harsh light or deep shadow… while smooth stone walls shoot even higher to a dome whose metallic interior is crowned by an oculus."[210] Visitors approach the spectacular five-story museum either by dhow from across the bay or by foot across a small bridge connecting the museum to the Doha Corniche. Once inside the building, one's gaze

---
(207) Benmayor, 2012.
(208) Abujbara, 2019.
(209) Kayahan, 2014.
(210) Crow, 2008.

is drawn upward toward the geometric apex and outward toward the shimmering Doha skyline, framed by a wall of glass. Fountains and other water features evoke the country's rich Islamic heritage, while the outdoor spaces of the museum afford visitors a stunning view of the landscape of the Doha Corniche.

The New York Times noted how the building "has emerged as one of the world's most encyclopedic collections of Islamic art" housed in a building that embodies the "essence of Islamic architecture."[211] The collection includes artifacts from three continents, spanning 1,400 years, and has helped showcase Qatar as a cultural center throughout the Middle East.

Tours of the Museum of Islamic Art take visitors on a journey beginning in the seventh century through the beginning of the twentieth century. There are displays of ceramic tiles and pottery, textiles, coins, manuscripts, woodwork, jewelry, armor, glass, and calligraphy from across the Muslim world-from Spain to India, Turkey, and China. The juxtaposition of priceless pieces from different cultures enhances the viewers' understanding of the evolution of the rich Islamic civilization over a broad span of time.

Sheikha Al Mayassa bint Hamad, the Chairperson of Qatar Museums, has led the museum in its quest to share knowledge of Islamic art in order to shape the future based on a deeper understanding of Islamic history. As a non-religious institution, the museum has been groundbreaking in terms of helping the world more deeply appreciate Islamic art and culture.

8.8. The New National Museum of Qatar

On March 28, 2019, the new, spectacular National Museum of Qatar opened its doors with a ceremony attended by the emir. This 560,000-square-foot, sand-colored museum is the embodiment of Qatar's national efforts to convert the country's gas wealth into a dialogue about Qatar's rich cultural heritage and its current and future aspirations.[212] Situated near Doha's airport highway, this multifaceted structure is one of the first sites that visitors see upon arrival and

---

(211) Ouroussoff, 2008.
(212) Sergie, 2019.

Chapter 8: Doha's Soft Power: Culture, Art and Museums

is one of Qatar's key attractions. The entrance alone includes 114 fountain sculptures and a roof composed of 76,000 panels.[213]

Sydney-based Koichi Takada Architects won the international competition to design the interior, while the exterior was designed by Pritzker Prize-winning French architect Jean Nouvel. "To construct a building 350 meters long, with its great big inward-curving disks, and its intersections and cantilevered elements—all the things that conjure up a desert rose—we had to meet enormous technical challenges," explained Nouvel. "This building is at the cutting-edge of technology, like Qatar itself." In the words of Takada, "The architecture is a representation of the desert rose mineral formation; a connection to nature… Each interior space offers a fragment of the Qatari history that aims to enhance and fulfill both a cultural and memorable experience for museum visitors."[214]

Costing roughly $434 million, the floor plan of the museum is a loop of 11 galleries with ceilings of shifting heights and asymmetrical, angular interior surfaces that engage the public in colorful and emotional ways.[215]

A meandering, multi-level, one-mile path takes approximately two hours to complete. At the beginning, a film covers the first 700 million years of life on this planet, accompanied by displays of fossils and models of the first animals. Galleries that follow cover life in Qatar from the beginning of human activity on the peninsula to the present. Maps, digital learning stations, texts, and archival photographs showcase Qatar's history.

A final walkway tells the story of the emirate's achievements from its past to the present. Visitors learn about pearl diving and traditional coffee making through films and dioramas. Dramatic tribal conflicts from Qatar's history are re-enacted on enormous screens. These stories include the rise of the ruling family to power and the emergence of the country's oil, and later natural gas, which would transform the emirate into an influential actor on the international stage.

---

(213) France24, 2019.
(214) Sergie, 2019.
(215) France24, 2019.

Suzanne Cords, a Deutsche Welle reporter, described the museum as a "utopian project" with a main objective "to trace the Gulf state's singular evolution from a small fishing community to a global economic powerhouse." She continued, "The story... is captured in the architecture that Jean Nouvel says encompasses the physical, human and economic geography of the country, as well as its history."[216]

The Art Newspaper, a leading industry publication, labeled the museum "breathtaking" and stated that "every aspect of modern museography is used to create immersive displays and engaging learning experiences." The reviewer added, "This is a 21st-century museum, which emphasizes the 3D experience in all its manifestations, but it also manages to have heart and soul...[it] reveals how vitally important it is for Qatar to preserve its history given the intense speed of social, political, and architectural change."[217]

The museum's design inspiration came from the forty-meter deep Cave of Light (Dahl al-Misfir), an underground sanctuary in central Qatar where rose-shaped gypsum deposits give off a phosphorescent glow. This geological phenomenon has come to be known as the 'desert rose'—hence, the evocative rose shape of the museum's exterior. In addition, the way the 'petals' of the desert rose structure wrapped around and enclosed the original palace of Sheikh Abdullah bin Jassim, which served as the first Qatar National Museum, creates a powerful connection between the past and the future.

8.9. Mathaf: Arab Museum of Modern Art

Co-owned by Qatar Museums and the Qatar Foundation, the Mathaf (Arab Museum of Modern Art) opened its doors in December 2010. It initially comprised a collection of Arab art established over two decades by Sheikh Hassan bin Mohammed Al Thani, an artist, art collector, educator, and member of Qatar's extended ruling family. Having amassed a collection as he traveled throughout the Middle East and beyond, Sheikh Hassan decided to create a museum to showcase and display his holdings, augmented by further pieces that offered an Arab perspective on modern and contemporary art. Housed in a former school building in Education City, Mathaf's

---
(216) Cords, 2019.
(217) Cole, 2019.

Chapter 8: Doha's Soft Power: Culture, Art and Museums

collection of more than 8,000 pieces traces the evolving trends in Arab art from the 1840s to the present. A series of temporary exhibitions complement the permanent exhibits and provides unique insight into modern Arab art. Mathaf additionally developed a research and educational component that encompassed the curation and publication of an Encyclopedia of Modernity and the Arab World. In 2015, Mathaf was shortlisted for the prize of 'best emerging cultural destination' in the Middle East by Leading Cultural Destinations, whose annual awards are sometimes described as the "Oscars" for museums around the world.[218]

8.10. Msheireb Museums

Located in four heritage houses in the historic center of Doha, the Msheireb Museums provide insight into the regeneration fueled by sudden oil wealth. The district underwent an earlier transformation with the renovation of the historic Souq Al Waqif in the 2000s. The Msheireb Museums comprise the Mohammed bin Jassim House, Company House, Radwani House, and the Bin Jelmood House, each concentrating on a different aspect of Qatar's history and heritage.

The Mohammed bin Jassim House was built by the son of Qatar's founder and features interactive and audio displays that chart the impact of the rapid socioeconomic changes of the mid-twentieth century. Company House was the first headquarters of the Qatari oil company, and its exhibits bring to life the early years of the oil industry. Radwani House examines the domestic life of a Qatari family between the 1930s and the 1960s and includes artifacts unearthed during archaeological excavations underneath the house, including an uncovered well and a limestone incense burner.[219]

Most attention has been focused, however, on the Bin Jelmood House, a remarkable museum that charts the history of slavery not only across the wider region but also in Qatar itself. Visitors who enter the Bin Jelmood House, named after former trader Mohammed Jelmood who lived in the house during the mid-twentieth century, are greeted by these words: "Bin Jelmood House exists to promote reflection and conversation on important truths about historical slavery in Qatar and the critical issue of contemporary slavery around

---
(218) D'Mello, 2015.
(219) Walker, 2016.

the world."[220] Slaves from East Africa once crowded into the courtyard of the house, and the museum does not shy away from covering the difficult legacies of the slave trade before its final abolition in the Middle East in 1952.

The Bin Jelmood House attracted widespread acclaim when it opened as the first museum in the Arabian Gulf that addressed taboo issues, from slavery to the current work conditions and the exploitation of workers. In fact, one of the panels at the house unabashedly tackles the contemporary issue of migrant worker abuse with a photograph of Nepalese workers on a Qatari construction site with accompanying text. It also illustrates examples of measures to address modern abuses, such as the banning of child camel jockeys in 2005 and the establishment of a safe house and rehabilitation center for women survivors of trafficking.

A 2016 article in The National, an Abu Dhabi newspaper, heralded the Bin Jelmood House as "a remarkable new museum in Doha [that] shines a rare light on the Indian Ocean slave trade a century ago, and is helping Qataris to shape their future by examining issues of race and identity in the Arab world."[221]

8.11. Qatar-USA Year of Culture 2021

In September 2020, during the annual U.S.-Qatar Strategic Dialogue, representatives from the two nations signed a memorandum of understanding marking 2021 as the "Qatar-USA Year of Culture." Subsequently, Qatar Museums and the Embassy of the United States in Doha launched a year-long program of cooperation intended to forge stronger ties between the two nations. As part of this effort, the United States and Qatar have initiated a series of complementary projects and events, particularly in the field of the arts.

Although the COVID-19 pandemic has impacted the events, the Year of Culture is slated to continue. It was initiated by a friendly match between the Washington Spirit women's football team and the Qatar national women's team, held on one of the new stadiums for the 2022 World Cup. The friendly match was immediately followed by musical performances by Arab singers and musicians and by members of the Qatar Philharmonic Orchestra.

---

(220) Ibid.
(221) Khan, 2016.

Going forward, the Year of Culture 2021 will continue with a yearlong series of meetings and seminars – particularly those working around the activities of the Fulbright program, the most widely recognized and arguably the most prestigious international exchange program in the world. Other events have included academic and professional seminars, sports tournaments, concerts featuring classical, jazz, and traditional Qatari music, and public art exhibitions.

8.12. Conclusion

For those who witnessed the Arabian Gulf half a century ago, its transformation has been nothing short of extraordinary. A population in which four in five men, and nearly all women, were once illiterate now enjoys education levels among the highest in the Arabic-speaking world and universities that rival in quality those of the traditional Arab centers of learning in the Levant. Once disdained as a cultural backwater, the Arabian Gulf today hosts a plethora of cultural centers, including museums, exhibits, art galleries, and a music and film industry that has a worldwide audience. More importantly, these institutions are not merely serving as conduits for the efforts of artists and intellectuals from elsewhere in the region. Instead, the citizens of the Gulf States themselves have taken on a major role in advancing the arts across the entire region.

Photography

The Doha skyline.

Qatar National Day celebration.

Doha Corniche landscape.

The Pearl-Qatar in Doha.

Souq Waqif, 1960s.

Souq Waqif today after renovation.

Photography

Qatar National Museum.

Museum of Islamic Art.

Katara Cultural Village Foundation.

Msheireb Museums.

Traditional folk music.

Bin Jelmood House in Doha.

Chapter 9
The Sports Hub of the Middle East

9.1. Introduction

Since the early 2000s, Qatar has pursued a national strategy to become both an international sports hub and a sports-minded country as essential building blocks of its national strategy. Beginning with two failed attempts to host the 2016 and 2020 Olympics, Qatar has dedicated itself to playing in the big league of sporting events. Qatar's blueprint for the future—its 2030 National Vision and its accompanying development strategy—explicitly includes sport as a vehicle through which Qatar can achieve its national goals.

Qatar hosted the 2006 Asian Games, a prelude to the 2008 Olympics, to prove its ability to host world-class sporting events. It has also hosted world squash and basketball championships as well as regional games in several sports.

However, Qatar has found its footing in association football, the world's most popular sport, and to general surprise won the bid to host the 2022 World Cup, the most important football tournament in the world.[222] It also won its bid to host the Doha 2030 Asian Games, which was voted on by the General Assembly of the Olympic Council of Asia on December 16, 2020, in the Omani capital, Muscat.

---

(222) "Association football" is the official name of the sport that is governed by the International Federation of Association Football (FIFA). This term is the origin of both "football" and "soccer," as the sport is known in North America, Australia, and southern Africa. Hereafter, the sport is referred to as "football."

Chapter 9: The Sports Hub of the Middle East

9.2. The Power of Sport

Sport is a powerful medium for the international spread of information, reputation, and relationships. The money spent worldwide on sports dwarfs the combined expenditures of all world governments on public diplomacy. Sports reflect the human quest for excellence, and its competition attracts the world's attention.

The size and dedication of the global audience for sports outnumbers the viewership for any other subject, including political affairs and movies. The drama of sports—the human striving for excellence and competition—captivates world attention. Consequently, the major powers of the world have spent tremendous sums to win in sports competitions as a major element of their national policy.[223]

Throughout their ancient and modern history, the Olympic Games, the most important sports tournament in the world, have been heralded as a force for world peace. During most of its ancient history, Greece called for general peace for several weeks before, during, and after the Games every four years. Competitors could journey safely, even through enemy cities, to and from the games. For a brief interval, foot races and javelin throws substituted for the clash of armies. It was no accident that the rebirth of the modern Olympic Movement in 1896, sponsored by Pierre de Frédy, Baron de Coubertin, grew out of the nineteenth-century European antiwar movement.[224]

The Cold War, more than any other time in sports history, elevated the Olympic Games as a proxy for great power competition. The Soviet Union, East Germany, and other Eastern Bloc countries built sports programs to prepare Olympic athletes for the games to demonstrate the superiority of the socialist system and as a way to bring the "joy of victory" to the home audiences and the "agony of defeat" to their political adversaries. The United States and other Western countries rose to the challenge. As the American ice hockey team's victory over the dominant Soviet Union in the Winter Games at Lake Placid in 1980 showed, victory in sport and patriotism were deeply intertwined.

---
(223) Sanders, n.d.
(224) Ibid.

Ultimately, while sports federations such as the IOC, FIFA, FINA, and others claim to be apolitical, they exist and work in a world of international politics. These federations form a society that transcends nationality, while they allow states to maneuver for national advantage.

Most crucially, the federations select the venue, city, and country to host events. For more than a century, countries have competed to be selected as hosts for the games, allowing the federations to exercise a power that is competitive with powerful states and amass wealth at the level of major international corporations. For the United States, sports play a different role in the country's outreach: they convey and confirm the American image as a land of opportunity and a meritocracy in which any individual, through talent and hard work, can excel and be rewarded. America's robust professional sports industry stays true to this value, irrespective of race or religion; teams and their fans only want to win. To gain an advantage, major American sports such as baseball and basketball hire from a worldwide pool of talent. The players in the widely televised American leagues are admired in the United States and elsewhere without regard to race or national origin.

9.3. Early Qatari Sports Ventures

As a new country, Qatar started late in developing its sports program in comparison with other Arab and Gulf states. The first sports club in the country was formed in 1948. In 1976, Qatar sent an administrative delegation to the Montreal Olympics, but it did not establish its own Olympic Committee (QOC) until 1979 to coordinate the participation of national teams and athletes at future international competitions.

Qatar's first official participation in the Olympics was at the 1984 Los Angeles Summer Games. Qatar participated with 27 athletes (all male) in three sports: athletics, football, and shooting. Qatar's participation in the opening ceremony of the Olympic Games and raising the national flag can be seen as a strategy of the Qatari government to assert its national autonomy on the global stage. The 1996 Atlanta Olympics gave Qatar another appearance on the American sports scene, but it gave little hint of what was to follow.[225]

---

(225) Reiche, 2014.

Chapter 9: The Sports Hub of the Middle East

In 1976, Qatar hosted the Gulf Cup, its first major regional sporting event of its own. Since then, it has continued to expand its sports footprint, hosting the Asian Football Cup in 1984, followed by a plethora of other sporting tournaments. Doha has been the site of numerous world and Asian championships in a diverse range of sports, including athletics, table tennis, and sailing. Doha also became the host of several annual sporting events, with an ATP tennis tournament being the first in 1993. In 2014 alone, Qatar set a record for hosting 57 international sporting events.[226]

By 2014, Qatar had won four Olympic bronze medals, all by men: the 1500-meter race in Barcelona 1992, weight lifting in Sydney in 2000, and shooting and high jumping in London in 2012. Qatar also hosted the 2015 World Handball Championships for men for the first time and became the first non-European country to win a medal.[227]

Qatar's three main sports administrative bodies—namely the Qatar Olympic Committee (QOC), the Ministry of Culture and Sports (MCS), and the Supreme Committee for Delivery & Legacy (SC)—oversee the national planning and delivery of sporting events. The QOC has a mandate to promote athletics and physical development and is responsible for coordinating and managing all Qatari bids to host the Olympic, Asian, and Arab Games. The QOC also organizes National Sports Day and operates the Qatar Olympic Academy and Qatar Women's Sports Committee.

In 2011, the Qatar Olympic Committee laid out three objectives for building a successful sports culture: (1) developing a healthy nation; (2) improving relations between nations; and (3) becoming a global sports hub. The MCS oversees all non-Olympic sports activities, including the country's 17 sports clubs and teams along with other sports federations. Lastly, the SC, which was formed in 2011, is responsible for the planning of the 2022 FIFA World Cup. This includes working with stakeholders to ensure that stadiums, infrastructure, and accommodations are in place for the event. Furthermore, the SC is responsible for ensuring a positive social and environmental legacy for the World Cup.[228]

---

(226) Reiche, 2014.
(227) Roy, 2020.
(228) Oxford Business Group, 2019

9.4. Qatari Sport Diplomacy

Qatar's leadership has greatly contributed to the interest, sponsorship, and support of sporting activities at home and hosting tournaments from abroad. Intense focus has been placed on football, which has a broad presence in and outside the Qatari community that goes beyond all other sporting activities.[229]

"Football diplomacy" in Qatar includes several elements and all work to enhance the Qatari presence on the global football stage. The most important tools are support for local talent among players and contracting with professionals in the Qatari League, as well as international investment, cooperation with international clubs, sponsorship of various teams and games, and competition for the right to host various international sports tournaments.[230]

The Qatari government has also made massive investments from the state's revenues in infrastructure in general and the construction and development of sports facilities in particular. Qatar has also invested in sports diplomacy indirectly by sponsoring sports competitions and sports clubs at the local, regional, and international levels. The Qatari leadership supported the advancement of sports diplomacy in Europe by purchasing or sponsoring first-class football teams and players. In addition to sports diplomacy, Qatari leaders see sports investment as part of a larger economic diversification strategy.[231]

This endeavor and Qatari initiatives have succeeded both internally and externally despite the well-organized and well-funded campaign by a number of Arab and foreign countries to deny Qatar the opportunity to host some international tournaments, such as the 2022 World Cup. What is most revealing is that the neighboring countries that imposed a blockade on the State of Qatar in 2017 did little to hide their desire to prevent Qatar from hosting the international event.

---

(229) Kum and Rusbad, 2018.
(230) Al-Amara, 2013.
(231) Mag, 2013.

Chapter 9: The Sports Hub of the Middle East

9.5. World Cup 2022

Qatar's greatest sports moment to date came on December 9, 2009, when FIFA President Joseph "Sepp" Blatter pulled the small country's name out of the winner's envelope announcing the award of the 2022 World Cup. Those watching the event on television noted Blatter's surprise that Qatar would host the games; it defeated the United States, which was heavily favored to win.

Qatar's 2022 country file, presented to FIFA before the decision, was distinguished by its use of new stadiums with a variety of designs, technology, and modern and environmentally-friendly innovations created to control the temperature in the stadiums, training areas, and stands. American companies, such as engineering firm AECOM, helped construct some of the World Cup stadiums. All of this was designed to allow players, administrators, and fans in the new stadiums to enjoy a cool and air-conditioned environment in the open air. Despite the intense heat of Qatar's desert during the summer, the air temperature inside the stadium would remain at approximately 27° C (80° F). To the disappointment of the Qataris, however, FIFA moved the date of the World Cup to the late fall, out of Qatar's summer season.

As another attractive feature of the Qatari bid, it included outreach to developing countries to provide football training for children and to dismantle some of the stadiums after the World Cup and move them to the developing world. Shortly thereafter, Qatar found itself the target of political attacks from all over the world. Some countries expressed discontent that the World Cup was awarded to a country from the Middle East. Qatar's regional rivals saw the award as strengthening their competitor. Most importantly, the award drew attention to the abysmal treatment of migrant workers in the wealthy GCC countries, and Qatar—which employed many such workers in building the infrastructure for the World Cup—became the main target for criticism.

Additionally, critics have raised doubts about Qatar's eligibility and ability to host international events due to its location in a region with many political conflicts and accused it of intolerance against other cultures. Qatar responded to its critics with concrete actions. The critics did not deter it from continuing its preparations for the World Cup by adhering to all standards and completing the construction of stadiums and the implementation of accompanying projects even before their official date.

Chapter 9: The Sports Hub of the Middle East

Qatar's increasing visibility in sport is not a new phenomenon or a product of coincidence; instead, it is evidence of a strategic approach that uses sports as a vehicle for development and public relations. The government of Qatar anticipates spending more than $60 billion on World Cup-related and legacy projects in the country's most significant international sports contest to date. This investment includes the completion of seven major stadiums and training sites. The government also plans to spend up to $140 billion to upgrade Qatar's infrastructure, especially the internal transportation network, in anticipation of the influx of tourists that the World Cup will create. World Cup-inspired investment projects include the new Doha Metro, an expanded highway system, and the redevelopment of Doha Port. The port will host cruise ships chartered to provide additional accommodation for the estimated 1.5 million fans expected to attend the event.[232]

In short, the 2022 World Cup will provide Qatar a historic opportunity to showcase its culture to the world, offering the country the chance to demonstrate its status as a sports powerhouse while building pride in Qatar as a nation. Having bested the United States as the host for the 2022 World Cup, Qataris have taken satisfaction with the United States hosting the next iteration of the games in 2026, along with Canada and Mexico.

9.6. Investment in the Domestic Sports Industry

In the past few years, Qatar has engaged in an aggressive campaign of investment in the global business of sports via its Qatar Sports Investment (QSI) fund. QSI was founded in 2005 as a joint initiative between the Qatar Olympic Committee and the Ministry of Finance. QSI has made key acquisitions in the sporting world, including the Paris Saint-Germain football club, a sportswear brand (BURRDA), various football television rights for Al Jazeera Sport, as well as the sponsorship of top European clubs such as FC Barcelona, estimated at 30 million euros per year from 2011 to 2016.

This strategy has proved fruitful. One example is the Qatar-based sports channel, Al Jazeera Sport, which now dominates the broadcasting rights of major sports competitions in the Middle East and North Africa (MENA). It extended its broadcast rights agreement

---

(232) Oxford Business Group, 2019

Chapter 9: The Sports Hub of the Middle East

with FIFA for the 2018 and 2022 FIFA World Cups in Russia and Qatar. The agreement covers cable, satellite, terrestrial, mobile, and broadband internet transmission across 23 territories and countries in the MENA region. The value of the deal was estimated to be approximately $1 billion. The channel is also expanding its market to Europe and the United States, competing with other major sports networks such as Canal+ and ESPN.[233]

While promoting sporting excellence, Qatar has also sought to commercialize its sporting ambitions internationally. Qatari companies including Qatar Airways, Qatar National Bank, and Ooredoo (Qatar's major telecoms company) have sponsored major European football clubs. Qatar Airways, for example, has long sponsored Germany's Bayern Munich and Italy's AS Roma.[234]

Qatar's local sports clubs devote huge financial resources to the building of state-of-the-art sports facilities and centers for elite sport development. It recruits foreign players and coaches to contribute to the development and performance of local leagues and national teams in major sports, particularly in team sports such as football, basketball, and volleyball.

Qatar's leadership, with the help of sports experts from all over the world, has made it a major goal to support the development of an elite sports program in the country. Aspire Sport Academy and ASPITAR (Qatar's Orthopedic and Sports Medicine Hospital) are two pillars of this elite development strategy that graduates a new generation of athletes at the professional level.

The investment in sports led to the emergence of national coaches, elite athletes, and sports administrators. The bronze medalist (high jump) for Qatar in the 2012 London Olympics, Mutaz Essa Barshim, was the first national who graduated from Aspire Academy to have won a medal in the Olympics. Moreover, Barshim added to his victory winning Qatar's first gold medal, the men's high jump, at the World Athletics Championships in Doha 2019. Recent data indicates that Qataris are now prominent competitors in an increasing number of sports, including handball,

---
(233) Amara, 2013.
(234) Oxford Business Group, 2019.

football, and volleyball. By present rankings, Qatar ranks 15th among 45 countries participating in the Asian Summer Games and first among the GCC countries.

In addition to the sports initiatives and projects at the national level, Qatar holds decision-making positions in regional, continental, and international sports organizations. The International Centre of Sport Security (ICSS) and the newly established Qatar Anti-Doping Laboratory promote Qatar as an international leader in the protection of international sports integrity, the fight against corruption, exploitation, and doping in sport.

The Doha GOALS (Gathering of All Leaders in Sports) forum is becoming an annual occasion to gather world leaders in politics, business, and media to talk about the power of sports in bringing cultures together. Former French president Nicolas Sarkozy, during the inaugural speech of 2012's forum, presented Qatar as a country where it is possible to reconcile faith, tradition, and modernity.[235] To this end, the Qatar Olympic and Sports Museum was recently launched to promote and protect the heritage of Arab sporting culture.

During the Olympic Games, the center organized an exhibition in the heart of London with the theme "Arab Women in Sport." This delivered a strong message to the international community that Qatar's heritage as an Arab and Muslim country does not preclude its welcoming of women in sport, with the IOC welcoming the participation of Qatari women in the Olympic Games.

9.7. Aspire Zone Sport City

Qatar's Aspire Zone Foundation, established by Emiri decree in 2008, brought together the organizations that grew out of Qatar's hosting of the 2006 Asian Games. Originally known as the Doha Sports City, Aspire Zone operates the Aspire Academy, ASPITAR, and Aspire Logistics.

Located in a 250-hectare sporting complex in Doha, Aspire Zone facilities include the Aspire Academy, opened in 2004 as an educational center for developing champions, a complex of sporting venues that served the 2006 Asian Games, and Doha's tallest

---

(235) Warshaw, 2012.

structure, the 300-meter Aspire Tower, housing The Torch Doha Hotel for visiting athletes and sports officials.

Additionally, the Zone contains the Aspire Dome, the world's largest indoor multipurpose dome with a total capacity of 15,500 seats that offers the highest quality facilities for multiple sports and international events.

Khalifa International Stadium, the most significant development in Aspire Zone, won the IOC/IAKS Distinction Award bronze medal in 2007. Now under renovation, the stadium will host some of the 2022 World Cup matches. The redevelopment includes modifications to ensure that the stadium complies with FIFA requirements, as well as innovative cooling technology to maintain an optimal temperature for players and spectators.

In October 2018, AZF and the Qatar Financial Centre (QFC) signed a memorandum of understanding that paved the way for the establishment of the Qatar Sports Business District (QSBD). The MoU matches AZF's twin areas of expertise in nurturing athletic ability and sports medicine with QFC's regulatory platform to create a sports business cluster, a first for the region. In line with the government's ambitions to increase foreign direct investment inflows, the new business district aims to attract multinational sports companies and start-ups through a range of incentives.

9.8. National Sports Day

Qatar's National Sports Day, the second Tuesday of every February, serves as an important annual occasion with the goal of engaging the local community in Qatar with sports activities and fostering the adoption of a healthy lifestyle. Qatar launched the first National Sports Day in 2012. Over the following years, the state enlisted government and private agencies to hold various events and activities and encourage citizens and residents to participate. Activities range from football to basketball, tennis to taekwondo, and cycling to swimming, with countless free sporting sessions and social competitions available to all ages and abilities in order to ensure that everyone has the opportunity to participate in sports.[236]

---

(236) Roy, 2020.

9.9. Sports Media

BeIN, Qatar's flagship sports network and a worldwide competitor for ESPN, is a global array of sports channels owned and operated by the beIN Media Group. Launched in France, the group currently operates channels in the Middle East and North Africa, France, Spain, the United States, Canada, Australia, New Zealand, Turkey, Hong Kong, Singapore, Malaysia, Indonesia, Philippines, and Thailand.

The other major Qatari sports station, which is widely watched at the local and Arab levels, was Al-Kass Sports Channel, based in Doha. Al-Kass was launched in June 2006 as the second Qatari sports channel, after Al-Jazeera Sports, which later became the BBC Sport group. The channel attracted many viewers with its unparalleled coverage of local sports, especially football. It also broadcast the 2006 Asian Games in Doha. The station has launched nearly eight sports channels, broadcasting around the world and around the clock.

9.10. Qatari-American Sports Collaboration

Qatar has made a special effort to draw in American participation at the 2022 World Cup. It has collaborated with popular American sports teams, broadcasters, and philanthropists to showcase Qatar's initiatives, build lasting partnerships, and educate American sports fans about Qatar. These initiatives have helped the Qatari Embassy reach major U.S. league sporting teams, their leadership, their fans, sports media, health organizations, donors, and more.

In 2019 and 2020, the Embassy brought roughly 500 children from the Washington, D.C. area to a curated venue to be a part of a day of fun with a health and wellness theme. In 2019, the Embassy partnered with the Washington Redskins (now the Washington Commanders), while in 2020, the Embassy expanded its partnership to also include DC United (the local professional men's soccer team), the Washington Spirit (the D.C. women's professional team), and the National Children's Museum.

Chapter 9: The Sports Hub of the Middle East

In partnership with DC United, DC Scores, the club's charitable arm, and the Supreme Committee for Delivery and Legacy, the Embassy co-hosted a "Soccer Fest" as part of DCU's home opening week-end. The exhibition included soccer-related activities, a "food village" of 16 local restaurants making Qatari-inspired dishes, a Qatari cultural exhibit, and a look into the preparations for the 2022 World Cup in Doha, Qatar. The celebration ultimately brought more than 2,000 fans a glimpse of what to expect from the Middle East's first World Cup.

On the margins of the public event, DC United hosted a VIP reception focused on building new partnerships with prominent individuals in the American soccer community, facilitating introductions for members of the Supreme Committee delegation with industry leaders, and showcasing the progress of the 2022 World Cup preparations in Doha.

The Embassy has had a longstanding partnership with the Washington, D.C. branch of America Scores, a non-profit dedicated to bringing soccer to schools in disadvantaged neighborhoods. The Embassy has made significant contributions to their after-school programs, and has adopted two of their elementary schools, funding their poetry and soccer programs entirely. Over the last two years, the Embassy has expanded its partnership with the national organization by hosting Qatar Sports Day activities with America Scores branches in New York and Los Angeles.

In 2019, Qatar expanded its partnership with America Scores New York by sponsoring four schools in Harlem and the Bronx. The Embassy has sponsored events to raise funds for the nonprofit, providing critical after-school soccer, literacy, and civic engagement programming at 20 sites in Harlem, Washington Heights, Inwood, the Bronx, and Brooklyn. The initiative extended to elementary and middle schools, as well as to high schools through the Kick it Forward program.

9.11. Conclusion

Although much of the discourse surrounding Qatar's global sporting ambitions are focused today on hosting the 2022 World Cup, the country has a long-term strategy to advance this vital sector on a local and international level. Doha's major investments in the global sports sector are aligned with a larger agenda aimed at ending the Qatari economy's dependence on the oil and energy sector and diversifying sources of income. By leveraging Qatar's wealth and political stability, its close ties with many governments around the world, and its reputation as an accepting and open society, officials in Doha are determined to make Qatar the capital of many future sports events that attract diverse fans from a myriad of countries, cultures, and nationalities. During the coming years, Qatar aims to obtain a greater share of the global sports market and actively bid on and organize international sporting events, helping it to play a major role in the international sports scene.

Photography

Announcement of the awarding of the 2022 FIFA World Cup to Qatar.

Asian Games opening ceremony, 2006.

Qatari stadiums constructed for the World Cup.

The logo of the upcoming World Cup.

Qatari national team celebrating their victory at the 2019 Asian Cup.

The Qatari Aspire Zone.

Photography

IAAF World Athletics Championships, held in Doha, 2019.

Qatar National Sport Day.

Qatar Football Association signs a cooperation agreement with its Moroccan counterpart.

H.E. Hassan Al Thawadi, Secretary General of the Supreme Committee for Delivery and Legacy.

Qatari women handball team.

Qatari sportswomen celebrate their 50M rifle prone triumph in the Doha Arab Games.

Chapter 10
The Qatari-American Strategic Partnership

10.1. Introduction

From the moment of its independence on September 1, 1971, Qatar was determined to develop a strong relationship with the United States. The United States officially recognized the State of Qatar on September 4 and established formal diplomatic relations on March 19, 1972, when American Ambassador William A. Stoltzfus, Jr. presented his credentials to the Emir of Qatar, Sheikh Khalifa bin Hamid Al Thani. At the time, Ambassador Stoltzfus, while living in Kuwait, was also accredited to all the other newly independent Gulf States.

After nearly a year of official communications, the United States Embassy in Doha was formally established on February 24, 1973, under Chargé d' Affaires ad interim John T. Wheelock. The first resident American Ambassador, Robert P. Paganelli, presented his credentials on August 22, 1974.

Qatar demonstrated the value it placed on the relationship with the United States by nominating its first Ambassador to the United States, Abdullah Saleh al-Mana', on June 22, 1972. Ambassador al-Mana' presented credentials on July 21, 1972, and opened the Qatari Embassy on the same day, seven months before the American Embassy opened in Doha.

From this beginning, the Qatari-American relationship has blossomed into an intricate, intimate, and mutually beneficial relationship across a broad spectrum of strategic sectors, whether policy, economic, societal, or simply personal. Qatar and the United States have forged a strategic alliance essential to maintaining America's presence, which the Gulf state governments deem essential to the stability of the Middle East and Indian Ocean basin.

Chapter 10: The Qatari-American Strategic Partnership

Economic ties are best defined by the multi-billion dollar investments each country has made in the other. American universities have embedded themselves in Qatar, while the Qatar Foundation International plays a significant role in improving American primary and secondary education. An estimated 40,000 Americans and their families live and work in Qatar,[237] while about 1,200 Qataris study each year in the United States. Finally, Qatar has modeled its political, economic, humanitarian, and educational aspirations on those of the United States.

10.2. Qatar's Embassy in Washington, DC

In 1972, Qatar opened its embassy in Washington, DC, as the fledgling state still strived to establish its diplomatic service. This first embassy was established along Wisconsin Avenue, near the National Cathedral, and was staffed by the ambassador, a handful of newly minted diplomats, and some locally hired Americans.. It soon moved to a small office building at 4200 Massachusetts Avenue on Washington's Embassy Row. Squeezed for space after it expanded its business and mission and increased its attaches and employees, the Embassy then moved in 2002 to a larger office space over a cinema at 4200 Wisconsin Avenue, in uptown Washington, DC.

The Embassy finally found a permanent home in 2005; moving to 2555 M Street on the edge of historic Georgetown. The Qatari Foreign Ministry renovated an old red brick building into an attractive, if small, embassy. As the Qatari-American strategic relationship has continued to grow, the embassy has expanded to incorporate a number of other buildings in its immediate vicinity and will soon have to find larger quarters.

In his first official visit to the United States in February 2015, Emir Sheikh Tamim chose the embassy as the podium from which to enunciate a clear message that has since been the foundation for strengthening the Qatar-U.S. partnership. He announced that Qatar was willing and able to play a pivotal role in ensuring stability and peace in the Middle East.

The current Qatari ambassador to the United States, Sheikh Meshal bin Hamad Al Thani, presented his credentials to President Donald Trump on April 24, 2017. Prior to this position, Ambassador Al Thani had served elsewhere in the United States and

---

(237) Snoj, 2019.

Chapter 10: The Qatari-American Strategic Partnership

was the Qatari Ambassador to France before taking up his duties in Washington. Similar to other diplomatic missions in Washington, the Qatar Embassy works with various organizations that support the strengthening of the Qatar-U.S. bilateral relationship, as well as many philanthropic missions.[238]

10.3. U.S.-Qatar Business Council

The U.S.-Qatar Business Council plays an important role in enhancing the Qatar-U.S. bilateral relationship. The Council, a private sector, non-profit, bilateral trade association, achieves this significant role by providing opportunities for discussion of key commercial and economic issues that are important to American companies doing business in Qatar and vice versa. The Council offers advisory and consultancy services, organizes trade missions for companies to facilitate bilateral business ties, and publishes weekly newsletters highlighting key events and developments in the Qatar-U.S. relationship.[239]

The U.S.-Qatar Business Council was founded in 1996 by the group of U.S. companies that first invested in the economy of Qatar after Sheikh Hamad came to power. Their goal was to promote economic, commercial, and trade relations between Qatar and the United States, which have grown exponentially ever since.

On its missions, the Council has hosted numerous high-ranking officials, including Fortune 500 executives, Emir Sheikh Tamim, and his father, Sheikh Hamad. Membership in the U.S.-Qatar Business Council is available to any organization or corporation registered in the United States and/or Qatar, and the Council provides many opportunities and benefits for its members. Members are given advice and counsel, appointments with business and government contacts in the United States and Qatar, and assistance for projects and programs.

The U.S.-Qatar Business Council recently opened its Qatar office at the end of 2019. At its opening ceremony, the president of the U.S.-Qatar Business Council, Anne Patterson, announced that "the Council is thrilled to be opening an office in Qatar and looks forward to extending its reach locally to the Qatari and American business

---

(238) Embassy of Qatar, 2020.
(239) US-Qatar Business Council, 2020.

community based here." This establishment will undoubtedly further enhance the economic cooperation and bilateral trade between the United States and Qatar.[240]

10.4. Qatar Foundation International

Located in Washington, DC, the Qatar Foundation International (QFI) is a subsidiary of QF that focuses on fostering a rich understanding of the Arab world. The organization partners with schools, multilateral entities, and other philanthropic organizations to teach the Arabic language and inform American students about Arab culture.

The organization's three main program areas, or pillars, are Connected Communities, Arab Societies and Cultures, and the Arabic language. QFI programs tend to cluster in poorer neighborhoods, such as the Bronx in New York and the South Side of Chicago. Most of the students come from disadvantaged backgrounds, and for them, the QFI programs expand their understanding of the world dramatically. Many of the QFI programs involve exchanges with a number of American students coming to Qatar to participate in programs such as mangrove swamp reconstitution, as an example. Other students, including those of two South Side Chicago high schools, participated in a larger program on water conservation at the Audubon Society in Washington, DC. In addition, a significant number of Qatari students participate with their American counterparts. In total, QFI operates more than forty programs in the United States and Canada with an additional 30 such programs in the United Kingdom, Germany, and Brazil.[241]

As the world becomes increasingly interconnected, QFI believes it is crucial to learn how to work with peers, not only in person but also online. The organization has many resources available to the public, including the online database Al Masdar, which aims to engage the community in facilitating connections. The open education research library provides a myriad of materials for teaching about the Arab world and the Arabic language.[242]

---

(240) The Peninsula, 2020.
(241) Qatar Foundation International, 2020.
(242) Qatar Foundation International, 2020.

10.5. Qatar America Institute for Culture (QAIC)

Qatar has also focused its outreach to the United States by encouraging and enabling cultural connections between the two countries. The Qatar America Institute for Culture (QAIC), an independent 501(c)3 nonprofit organization located in Washington, DC, was established in 2017 with Qatari financial support and leadership.

The Institute seeks to expand the cultural and artistic links between the two countries through authentic experiences such as exhibitions, cultural dialogues, fellowships, and other artistic initiatives. In recognition of the artistic contributions and talent of Qatar's large expatriate population that draws heavily from the countries of the Middle East, North Africa, and South Asia, it also offers programs focusing on the wider Arab and Islamic worlds.

At its headquarters in Washington's historic DuPont Circle neighborhood, QAIC hosts a regular series of culinary events, film festivals, and educational activities that introduce elements of Qatari culture to a largely American audience. They have included photography competitions, Arab-specific film awards, and an exquisite perfumery museum. Over the past four years, QAIC has added over four thousand people to its growing network and has featured more than five hundred artists and scholars from the region.

As QAIC's Executive Director since 2019, Fatima Al-Dosari has spearheaded activities that spotlight and celebrate the often overlooked and under-appreciated cultural commonalities between the two countries. Qatar's ongoing support for this independent non-profit evinces a non-traditional approach to engaging with the world, which has almost always been through ministries and state-owned entities.

This approach highlights its conviction that international relations go beyond traditional diplomacy and can be strengthened through consistent and long-term investments in the cultural sphere and others that allow it to project soft power. As evidenced by its support for QAIC, Qatar fundamentally believes that people build relationships. Qatar's commitment to hosting the 2022 World Cup tournament provides further evidence of this approach.

---

(243) Qatar America Institute, 2020.
(244) CNN, 2005.

10.6. Qatari Humanitarian Activity in the United States

Qatar's first recorded humanitarian efforts in the United States began with a $1 million gift from then-Emir Sheikh Hamid to New York City during his November 2001 visit after the 9/11 attacks. A few days later, the emir hosted a meeting of American Muslim leaders in Washington and, during the discussion, asked if any place of worship had been damaged or destroyed in the 9/11 attacks. After he learned that the collapse of the Twin Towers had destroyed an old Greek Orthodox Church at Ground Zero, the emir immediately directed a grant for its rebuilding.

Qatar's humanitarian assistance to the United States gained recognition and wide appreciation in 2005 when Qatar donated $100 million for relief and reconstruction in the wake of the disaster following Hurricane Katrina.[244] Although Qatar was not alone in its donation during this crisis, it remained uniquely involved in the recovery process by creating grants for specific organizations and institutions which, by 2006, totaled an additional $60 million.[245] Qatar took a different tack than most other donors; it did not simply turn over its money to the U.S. Government for FEMA or to other organizations but reached out to those most affected. Much of Qatar's effort was focused on higher education, giving $10 million to Tulane University and $17.5 million to Xavier University, a historically Black and Catholic institution, both of which had been damaged in the disaster. The State Department removed Qatar from its website list of foreign countries coming to the assistance of New Orleans because the Department did not get the aid exclusively, although Qatar was the second-largest foreign donor. In fact, Qatar was the only donor that ultimately spent more than it pledged.

In 2008, the Qatari emir took a two-day tour of the region to witness the impact of the grants.[246] In 2015, a decade after Hurricane Katrina, Qatari officials held a "celebration of recovery" in New Orleans with local dignitaries to celebrate Qatar's role in the recovery of the region and to launch a book documenting Qatar's efforts with stories from the beneficiaries of Qatar's $100 million in grants.[247]

---

(245) Strom, 2006.
(246) Pope, 2008.
(247) Ahmed, 2015.

Chapter 10: The Qatari-American Strategic Partnership

In 2017, Qatar provided $30 million in grants and aid for recovery after Hurricane Harvey hit the American South. It has also doled out donations to aid in the U.S. COVID-19 response. Qatar's aid to the United States in response to the pandemic included $1 million to Florida, $5 million to Los Angeles, and a similar amount to New York, prompting a grateful tweet from Governor Andrew Cuomo.[248]

Qatar has frequently contributed to smaller, lesser-known but important charitable and humanitarian causes in the United States. In early 2021, Qatar's Ambassador to the United States, Sheikh Meshal bin Hamad Al Thani, announced donations to several American organizations throughout the United States in recognition of World Autism Day and Autism Awareness Month. The donations were to charities such as the Dan Marino Foundation, Touro University, Break the Barriers, the Westview School, the Organization for Autism Research (OAR), and NEXT for AUTISM. These charities support the autistic community and their families, promote a message of acceptance and understanding, and bolster research into innovative new treatment methods and therapies. The donations from the Embassy were used to establish the Qatar Patient Care fund, supporting therapy services for children with autism. In 2019, Touro alone had more than 5,800 patient appointments, and as therapy services return to post-pandemic levels, the group will hire additional therapists and increase the number of families served.

The Embassy has also developed an educational program called the "Embassy Adoption Program" (EAP), in collaboration with the District of Columbia Public School System (DCPS) and Washington Performing Arts. The EAP partners different nations' embassies from across the world with various fifth and sixth grade classes and exposes them to the customs, cultures and languages of various nations. The goal is to encourage "global citizenry, curiosity, and empathy." The DCPS system is one of the most disadvantaged in the country; many of its students are recent immigrants, or come from economically disadvantaged backgrounds, and would not ordinarily have any exposure to a country like Qatar.

---

(248) Embassy of Qatar, 2020; Day, 2020; Middle East Monitor, 2020

Chapter 10: The Qatari-American Strategic Partnership

Roughly 80 Embassies from around the world, all of which were conveniently located in Washington, D.C., participated alongside Qatar in the 2017-2018 school year. This program has provided an opportunity to expose American youth to unfamiliar cultures, foster long-term goodwill, and combat negative notions of foreign culture.

The Embassy gives special attention to its outreach to the District of Columbia. Every year, the Embassy joins the DC Metropolitan Police Department to host a back-to-school celebration in Washington, DC's third ward, the poorest sector of the city. The engagement, which encourages children to enjoy a final active day of summer before the school year, also prepares them for the year ahead by providing needed supplies, and introduces disadvantaged students to the educational and tutor resources available to them. It also introduces parents to the various childcare services and educational programming available after school for their children. In the last three years, the Embassy has donated more than one thousand backpacks with school supplies to the local community.

The Embassy initiated a relationship with the Boys and Girls Clubs of America Partnership (BGC) in 2007 after the devastation of Hurricane Katrina, supporting the rebuilding of their destroyed club in New Orleans. While the relationship with the Boys and Girls Clubs declined after the initial donation, the Embassy began to restore the partnership roughly five years ago by making contributions to the local Washington, D.C. chapter, and hosting regular events alongside the organization. Since then, the Embassy has hosted an annual Qatar Sports Day celebration with the club in February, and a Qatar Spring Festival with the children in April. In 2019, these events were hosted in Boys and Girls Clubs across the United States, in cities including Los Angeles, Miami, New Orleans, New York City, and Tampa.

A notable trend in Qatar's history of humanitarian aid to the United States is its level of active engagement with relief projects. Qatari aid to help the U.S. recover from crises is often aimed at providing grants or building specific projects that focus on addressing problems at the community level and helping them rebuild important institutions in the region affected by the crisis, rather than simply giving money to the U.S. government, which might use it less efficiently.

10.7. Qatar Investment Authority

Given the small country's status as the world's second-largest exporter of natural gas, it should not come as a surprise that Qatar has perhaps the highest per capita GDP in the world. Prior to the COVID-19 pandemic, the government budget regularly ran large surpluses. To maximize the value of these funds, then-Emir Sheikh Hamad established the Qatar Investment Authority (QIA) to invest surplus capital both domestically and abroad. QIA operates as a sovereign wealth fund for the State, with an estimated $335 billion in assets as of 2019. In early 2019, QIA released preliminary plans to raise investments in the United States by more than $45 billion in the following two years. The CEO of QIA, Mansour Ibrahim Al-Mahmoud, reaffirmed that this commitment would focus on key sectors of investment in the United States, such as real estate, technology, and U.S. stock exchanges. QIA opened its New York City office in 2015 in order to promote and better manage these investments.[249]

Trade between Qatar and the United States has expanded at an exponential rate over the past decade. Prior to 1995, American exports to Qatar never exceeded $200 million annually, and Qatar never exported more than $80 million. American exports exploded as the LNG facilities came online, and by 2019, bilateral trade between the two countries had expanded to $8.152 billion. This balance has always favored the United States, which sold $4.76 billion more than it bought in the latest annual figures from 2019.[250] Although estimates of export-generated jobs are never precise, exports to Qatar are thought to keep 100,000 or more Americans at work.[251]

10.8. Qatari Diar Investment Group

The heightened economic relationship between America and Qatar began in 2010, when the Qatari Diar investment group, an affiliate of the QIA, announced its $700 million investment in CityCenterDC, a massive high-end urban development project in the nation's capital.

Qatari Diar was established in 2005 by the QIA and has rapidly expanded its international portfolio in the years since. According to Diar's website, the investment group has two projects in the United States, both of which are located in DC. First, its investment in the

---

(249) Parasie, 2015.
(250) United States Census Bureau, 2020.
(251) International Trade Administration, 2020.

CityCenterDC project kicked off the group's investments in the U.S. real estate market in 2010. The project was widely seen as the first of its kind, prompting some discussion about whether funding bars and conventional banks is compliant with Islam. Qatari Diar rejected the idea that special accommodations were made, stating that there were no such conflicts in the CityCenterDC plans from the beginning. The project was largely completed in 2013, and the development continues to be home to many high-end shops and restaurants.[252]

This new significant investment from Qatar into the Washington, DC, real estate market caught the attention of DC officials and further strengthened the business relationship between Qatar and the city. This development culminated in 2017 when a group of DC officials and businesspeople visited Qatar to encourage more investment in DC real estate, despite the emerging Gulf crisis at the time.[253]

In 2019, Qatari Diar completed a $250 million development project on DC's Conrad Hotel. Most transactions have happened through third-party investors with close ties to the Qatari government, but the government became directly involved when the Qatari embassy bought Hollerith House for $17.75 million in April 2020.[254]

10.9. Private Qatari Investments in the U.S.

The Qatari private sector came late to the game in the United States. Some family firms such as Al Mannai had invested in the Houston, Texas, area in the 1970s but withdrew after a domestic market downturn in the early 1980s.

Private Qatari investments did not reappear in the United States until Qatari Diar opened its project in Washington, DC. Following its lead, private Qatari investment groups have recently invested significant sums in New York, Washington D.C., Miami, and Chicago real estate.

The Al Faisal Group has, over the last ten years, developed Chicago's Radisson Blu Aqua Hotel, followed by the acquisition of St. Regis in Bal Harbor, Florida, St. Regis in Washington, DC, W Hotel in Miami, and Manhattan at Times Square Hotel in New

---
(252) Fisher, 2017.
(253) Goff, 2017.
(254) United States Census Bureau, 2020.

York.²⁵⁵ Other private sector firms have joined in the recent surge, primarily in luxury hospitality projects. In 2015, Al Rayyan Tourism Investment Co bought the St. Regis hotel in Washington, DC.

The next year, Al Sraiya Holding Group bought the Club Quarters hotel for $52.4 million.²⁵⁶ After that, Alduwaliya Hospitality bought the Homewood Suites and also purchased a twelve-story office building on Connecticut Avenue NW for $64 million and a building on Thomas Jefferson Street for $142 million, both in DC.²⁵⁷

In addition to Qatari Diar's expensive development projects in the United States, other Qatari firms have invested billions into real estate nationwide. In New York City, Qatari investment groups, working with the sovereign wealth funds, purchased the InterContinental Barclay Hotel for $300 million, in addition to buying a stake in several major real estate trusts like Empire Realty Trust that includes the Empire State Building and Manhattan West, valued at $8 billion.²⁵⁸ In Los Angeles, Qatar purchased a $1.3 billion office portfolio from the Blackstone Group in 2016, opening up its investment in the West Coast.

10.10. University Programs and Think Tanks

The Qatar Foundation for Education, Science and Community Development funds programs at universities and offers additional scholarships and financial aid for students.

Between 2012 and 2018, Qatar gave millions of dollars to institutions in the United States and the United Kingdom. Qatar's contribution represented nearly 15 percent of all foreign funding over that period. Qatar alone funded $1.3 billion of the $2.2 billion from all Gulf countries combined.²⁵⁹

American commentators and political activists have expressed concerns about the motives behind Qatar's generous funding. Some argue that Doha is attempting to increase its political influence in Washington by funding universities such as Georgetown, "which is

---

(255) International Trade Administration, 2020.
(256) Fisher, 2017.
(257) Goff, 2017.
(258) Al-Arabiya, 2018.
(259) Ibid.

situated in the seat of power and... frequently cited by groups shaping policy."[260] Qatar insists that its efforts in the field of education, as the experiences of recent years prove, are not focused on politics and its details but aim to support academic programs in American universities and build a better understanding between the Middle East and the West.

Qatar is also no stranger to American think tanks, donating $14.8 million to the Brookings Institution and establishing an affiliated Brookings center in Qatar.[261] Qatar also has a deep relationship with the RAND Corporation. Qatar and RAND established the RAND-Qatar Policy Institute, which ended in 2013 and produced a plethora of research projects focused on Qatari issues, especially education.[262]

10.11. Diplomats Who Have Contributed to the Qatari-American Relationship

This section seeks to recognize and commemorate the ambassadors and diplomats who have worked to deepen Qatar-U.S. bilateral ties. On the Qatari side, they include: H.E. Abdullah Salah Al-Mana (1972-1980), H.E. Abdul-Kader Bareek Al-Amari (1981-1987), H.E. Ahmed Abdullah Al-Mahmoud (1987-1989), H.E. Dr. Hamad Abdelaziz Al-Kuwari (1990-1993), H.E. Sheikh Abdelrahman Bid Saoud Al-Thani (1993-1997), H.E. Saad Mohammed Al-Kabeesi (1997-2000), H.E. Badr Amr Al-Dafe (2000-2005), H.E. Nasser Hamad Al-Khalifa (2005-2007), H.E. Ali Fahad Al-Hajri (2008-2011), H.E. Mohammed Abdullah Al-Rumaihi (2012-2013), H.E. Mohamad Jaham Al Kuwari (2013-2016), H.E. Sheikh Meshal Bin Hamad Al-Thani (2017-).

The following U.S. ambassadors also contributed to the enduring strength of the Qatar-U.S. partnership. They include: William Stoltzfus (1972-1974), Robert Peter Paganelli (1974-1977), Andrew Ivy Killgore (1977-1980), Charles E. Marthinsen (1980-1983), Charles Franklin Dunbar (1983-1985), Joseph Ghougassian (1985-1989), Mark Gregory Hambley (1989-1992), Kenton Keith (1992-1995), Patrick N. Theros (1995-1998), Elizabeth Davenport McKune (1998-2001), Maureen E. Quinn (2001-2004), Chase Untermeyer

---
(260) Rosiak, 2018.
(261) Lipton et.al., 2018.
(262) RAND Corporation, 2020.

(2004-2007), Joseph LeBaron (2008-2011), Susan L. Ziadeh (2011-2014), Dana Shell Smith (2014-2017), Chargé d'Affaires Greta C. Holtz (2020-2021), Chargé d'Affaires John Desrocher (2021-).

10.12. Conclusion

Qatar has a deep, abiding relationship with the United States that spans almost every sector. The two nations maintain excellent geostrategic, economic, business, humanitarian, and social partnerships.

The strong bonds between Qatar and the U.S. grew from very little. During the period of British protection, London tightly controlled diplomatic access from the American government and permitted only the consular officer at Dhahran to visit on a regular schedule, a practice that continued until 1971. One of the co-authors was assigned as the "circuit-riding" American Vice Consul to the Trucial States from 1964 to 1966. He visited Doha on a regular monthly schedule, and was required to work from the British Political Agency, and was told to have no contact with the Qataris themselves. In 1995, the U.S. had five diplomatic staff on hand to manage Washington's relations with Qatar.

Washington's political calculus changed after the 1990 Iraqi invasion of Kuwait. Qatar, which had generally looked to its larger neighbor, Saudi Arabia, for protection, realized Riyadh was unable to defend itself against aggression; ultimately, Doha realized it needed to call the Americans, and Qatar rapidly forged stronger ties to the U.S.

Qatar not only bases its national security on a solid partnership with the United States but has also chosen to treat the American experience in education, human rights, economic development, and political evolution as a guiding light for its own development. The two countries began their history in completely different places, and each has its own circumstances to evolve; Qatar has not simply imitated what the United States does. However, there is no doubt that the two countries share the same end goals, although they clearly cannot be achieved at the same pace and timetable. One might argue that Qatar's pace, starting 200 years after the United States, has been much faster. If this is true, it is only because the United States provided the small, young peninsular nation a clear example to work from. America and Qatar's fruitful partnership continues to improve; as it does, it promises to benefit both countries and the greater region as well.

Photography

Sheikh Hamad contributing to the rebuilding of New York folliwing the 9/11 attacks

Sheikh Hamad visiting Louisiana after Hurricane Katrina. Qatar donated $100 million to the relief effort.

A commemorative book describing the work of the Qatar Katrina Fund.

Sheikh Tamim visiting the White House in 2018, following the onset of the Gulf diplomatic crisis in June 2017.

The Qatar-USA Year of Culture 2021.

Qatari sportswomen celebrate their 50M rifle prone triumph in the Doha Arab Games.

Photography

Qatari real estate development projects in U.S. cities, including Washington, DC.

Qatar-U.S. sign agreements.

Qatar Airways celebrating the launch of its freighter service to Miami.

A U.S.-Qatar Business Council meeting.

Qatar America Institute in Washington, DC, hosting a celebration of the 2022 World Cup.

U.S.-Islamic World Forum in Doha.

Photography

The United States Embassy headquarters in Doha.

Embassy of Qatar headquarter in Washington, DC.

Qatari volunteers, after the nation's commitment to donating 27,000 meals during Ramadan.

U.S.-Qatar Annual Strategic Dialogue

Qatari Ambassador to the U.S. receives Medal for Distinguished Public Service, 2021.

Trevor Noah speaks at the Qatar Autism Gala, 2018.

Photography

His Excellency Mr. Abdullah Salah Al-Mana
Ambassador
1972 – 1980

His Excellency Mr. Abdul-Kader Bareek Al-Amari
Ambassador
1981 – 1987

His Excellency Mr. Ahmed Abdullah Al-Mahmoud
Ambassador
1987 – 1989

His Excellency Mr. Dr. Hamad Abdelaziz Al-Kuwari
Ambassador
1990 – 1993

His Excellency Mr. Sheikh Abdelrahman Bin Saoud Al-Thani
Ambassador
1993 – 1997

His Excellency Mr. Saad Mohammed Al-Kabeesi
Ambassador
1997 – 2000

Photography

His Excellency Mr. Badr Amr Al-Dafe'
Ambassador
2000 – 2005

His Excellency Mr. Nasser Hamad Al-Khalifa
Ambassador
2005 – 2007

His Excellency Mr. Ali Fahad Al-Hajri
Ambassador
2008 – 2011

His Excellency Mr. Mohammed Abdullah Al-Rumaihi
Ambassador
2012 – 2013

His Excellency Mr. Mohamed Jaham Al Kuwari
Ambassador
2013 – 2016

His Excellency Sheikh Meshal Bin Hamad Al-Thani
Ambassador
2017 – Current

Conclusion

Two centuries ago, the small Arab sheikhdoms of the Gulf region played no important role in global politics. Throughout their history, Turks, Persians, and several different European nations fought over control of the Gulf ports and land. The societies that lived in the region depended on the resources of transit trade, hunting, pastoralism, and primitive agriculture.

The only local product with export value was the pearl, whose trade flourished in an early golden period but whose time ended with the invention of the Japanese cultured pearl and the global economic depression. While some local merchants and foreign businessmen who exported it to Europe and the United States benefited from the pearl trade, it provided a poor livelihood for those who risked their lives to dive and collect it from the sea.

Even after the Second World War, the small Arab states of the Gulf languished under foreign "protection," with almost no voice in determining their future and lacking even the minimal tools to improve their societies and economies. Fate, however, intervened in the discovery of unimaginable oil wealth at a time when wars had so devastated the foreign "protector" that it had lost the means and the will to impose its control. The smaller Gulf States emerged at this time, and over half a century, they have secured a level of well-being beyond their wildest expectations.

The State of Qatar, through a serendipitous combination of the grit and wisdom of its people and leadership, has transformed itself

Conclusion

from an obscure nation with little economic and political capacity into a powerful and respected force around the world. Qatar preserved its independent identity by striking international and regional deals and agreements to protect its interests and use its wealth.

American-Qatari relations started in the early 1930s, when several American oil companies sought to negotiate oil exploration deals directly with Qatari leadership, bypassing the British. Unlike all other Western governments, the first Americans in Qatar came to do good deeds rather than to profit financially or politically. The American Protestant Mission in Bahrain responded to an appeal and opened a small hospital in Doha that later became a healthcare hub in the Middle East.

Thus, from the very first days of creating its modern state, Qatar sought closer ties with the United States. But these efforts were challenged with Washington prioritizing relations with Saudi Arabia and Iran, the two major powers in the Gulf, and largely ignoring the smaller states (except for Kuwait). This policy provoked the first diplomatic dispute between the two countries in 1988 when Qatar managed to obtain Stinger missiles from the black market—a step that angered the Americans until it was resolved a few years later.

Qatar, however, sought to strengthen its relations with the United States, even during crises. Doha began to build bridges to Washington by sending students to the United States and attracting American oil companies. After Qatar participated in the liberation of Kuwait from the Iraqi invasion, the bilateral relationship began to grow at an accelerated pace.

Over the past 32 years and through the challenging events of September 11, the War on Terror, the invasions of Afghanistan and Iraq, and the post-Arab Spring period, Qatari-American relations have blossomed at all levels: political, economic, defense, and even educational. Today, Qatar hosts some of the most important U.S. military facilities abroad. Al Udeid Airbase, an airbase Qatar built "on spec," serves as the key logistical hub for all U.S. military operations in the Middle East and western Asia. The United States has transferred the forward headquarters of U.S. Central Command, the military organization responsible for the entire region, to Al Udeid. This has made Qatar an indispensable ally.

Conclusion

Qatar's decision to build a partnership with Mobil, an American oil company, also reflected Qatari conviction that the United States provided the highest quality technology and the resources to develop the North Dome Gas Field, the world's largest. This partnership has made Qatar the largest exporter of liquefied natural gas in the world. Natural gas brings another important benefit as well; given that it produces 40 percent less carbon dioxide than any other fossil fuel, it will play a key role in the transition to the carbon-neutral economy of the future, mitigating the damage of climate change.

Eager to hold up its side of the Qatari-American relationship, Doha came to the assistance of the United States after disasters such as Hurricane Katrina and provided $100 million to aid the reconstruction of New Orleans. Doha continues to provide aid to the United States and other parts of the Americas through the COVID-19 crisis.

Qatar's experience proves there is no preordained path to progress. Many in the West believe that the common principles dictated by the West's particular history represent the only way to democracy, human freedom and prosperity. Western governments have invested enormous human resources and wealth to educate, persuade, cajole, and sometimes coerce other countries to copy Western models as the only way to progress. In doing so, the west often loses sight of the final objective. Government with the consent of the governed, buttressed by the rule of law, is a universal good that can be achieved by means other than copying a Western constitution and foreign governing mechanisms.

The Qatari system of government has adopted many of the best practices of the Western liberal democracies, imported the best educational institutions, and aligned with the best financial practices. Despite this, it has not abandoned its traditions or erased its past. Rather, Qatar has retained the best features of its traditional tribal society, most important being governance by consultation and consensus. Progress has come at a slow but steady pace, with an occasional misstep, but generally Qatar has moved forward.

Conclusion

On the issue of human rights, Qatar has managed to achieve Western standards over the short span of four to five decades. After an international outcry, Qatar voluntarily abolished the detestable kafala system and raised the status of its foreign workers from what could arguably be described as modern slavery to a status similar to that of a gastarbeiter in postwar Germany. It took the United States three centuries and a bloody civil war to do the same for its former slaves and another century to bring them to full legal equality. And, like the United States, Qatar knows that it still has much work to do.

Moreover, unlike other countries that have equated great wealth and power, the Qataris have shown that they understand their wealth is only a means to an end. They know that an educated and involved youth adds more value than any amount of oil and gas. Qataris learned from centuries of lived experience that their security rests on making the country valuable to powerful but distant states. The country has forged strong ties through business, education, sports, and humanitarian activities with the major powers of the world, especially the United States, and continues to cultivate those ties assiduously.

Qatar leads the region in ensuring that its graduates, particularly women, find productive employment after graduation. Elsewhere in the region, huge numbers of unemployed college graduates fester in frustration due to a lack of high-skilled jobs. Qatar understands that those same young people will not be satisfied with material goods at state expense but will insist on participating in decisions that affect their collective lives. Therefore, the introduction of a free press, a municipal council, and ultimately a constitution and an elected legislature was brought about by Qatar's ruling family, even though it may lose a measure of its political power in the process.

Qatar has not copied the "human rights development" pattern in neighboring countries that, on the one hand, grant social freedoms by monarchical fiat and, on the other, continue to jail those who advocate for them. It recognizes that sustaining social and political progress at home requires helping to propagate it abroad. Al Jazeera and Qatar's many conferences on human rights, tolerance, and democracy have represented a genuine, if not entirely successful, effort to plant that same seed in the region.

Conclusion

Like all other human endeavors, progress in Qatar has been uneven, but the country's leadership has never lost sight of the understanding that a free and empowered population counts more for the future security and prosperity of their nation than skyscrapers, mansions, yachts, and other manifestations of wealth.

Most importantly, Qatar has demonstrated that it understands the importance of its strong relationship with the United States. Despite their differences in size and political power, the relationship between the United States and Qatar is not that of a patron and a client. Qatar shares America's regional objectives, but it will caution against what it believes are mistakes on Washington's part. It will also take risks on America's behalf, rather than expecting Washington to shoulder the burden alone. It contributes where America cannot and deploys its own influence for a common purpose, even when others will not.

In the end, critics may argue that without the good luck of ruling over the world's largest natural gas deposit none of Qatar's developments would have come to fruition. Certainly, the wealth that made Qatar the richest country per capita on Earth made these developments possible. However, good leadership was also essential; other supremely wealthy states, including several of Qatar's neighbors, have fumbled similar advantages, despite their larger size and population, well-developed militaries, and proximity to the centers of world power. Qatar has not repeated these mistakes; aided by its enormous wealth, it has created a flawed but fundamentally workable society, taking the best from its traditions and Western influence to create a strong, modern, and progressive state.

Bibliography

Abujbara, A. (2019). "Simple, Iconic: How I.M. Pei's Museum of Islamic Art Reshaped Qatar." Retrieved from: www.aljazeera.com.

Ahmed, A. (2015). "Qatar Really Wants You to Know How Much It Gave for Katrina Relief." Retrieved from: www.huffpost.com.

Al Arabiya TV. (2018). "How Qatar is Paying U.S. Institutions $1.3 Billion to Gain 'Dubious Influence.'" www.english.alarabiya.net.

Al Faisal Holding. (2020). "Al Rayyan Tourism Investment Company." www.alfaisalholding.com.

Al Jazeera Network. (2017). "NHRC: Qatar Blockade Worse than Berlin Wall." www.aljazeera.com.

Al Jazeera Network. (2019). "Qatar National Museum Set to Open Doors to the Public." www.aljazeera.com.

Al Jazeera (2021). "Qatar Lauded for Its Role in Afghanistan Evacuations." Retrieved from: www.aljazeera.com.

Al-Ezzi, K. (1972). The Arab Gulf in Its Past and Present. Baghdad: Al-Jahiz Press.

Al-Duwaish, S. (2013). "Common Civilization Features between the Qatar Peninsula and John of Kuwait from the Fifth Millennium BC to the End of the Iron Age." KSA: King Abdulaziz House of Publication.

Al-Ghanim, K. (1994). Group Celebrations and Some Accompanying Cultural Forms in the Diving Community. Qatar: Ministry of Culture Publication.

Al-Jaber, K., Auter, P., & Arafa, M. (2003). "Audience Perceptions of Al-Jazeera TV." In P. Auter (Chair), Al-Jazeera TV: What Type of Voice for the Arab World? Panel sponsored by the Radio TV Jour-nalism Division at the national convention of the Association for Educators in Journalism and Mass Communication, Kansas City, MO.

Bibliography

Al-Jaber, K., Auter, P., & Arafa, M. (2005). "Hungry for News and Information: Instrumental Use of Al-Jazeera TV Among Viewers in the Arab World and Arab Diaspora." Journal of Middle East Media, 1(1), 21-50.

Al-Jaber, K. & Elareshi, M. (2016). "The New Media as Alternative Medium in the GCC Region: the Growing Influence of Social Networks." In B. Gunter, M. Elareshi, & K. Al-Jaber (Eds., Social Media in the Arab World: Communication and Public Opinion in the Gulf States. London: I.B Tauris Publishers.

Al-Jaber, K. & Gunter, B. (2013) Evolving news systems in the Gulf countries, Gunter, B. and Dickinson, R. (eds) News media in the Arab world. New York: Bloomsbury.

Al-Kafarneh, A. (2019). The Tribe in the Arab Political System. Jordan: Al-Balqa University Press.

Al-Kuwari, M. (2015). "Qatar Katrina Fund is a Tale of Friendship." Retrieved from: www.nola.com.

Allison, M. and Shaw, S. (1994). Doctor Mary in Arabia: Memoirs. Austin, TX: University of Texas Press.

Al-Maadheed, F. (2017). "Qatar: Past, Present, and Prospects for Education." In Education in the Arab World. London: Bloomsbury.

Al-Marikhi, S. (1996). The Economic Life of Qatar from the Emergence of Islam until the End of the Fourth Century AH. Qatar University Press.

Al-Qubaisi, N. (2007). "Trade and Money in the State of Qatar during the Islamic Ages." Journal of the College of Arts. Iraq: University of Baghdad Press.

Al-Rumaihi, A. (2012). "Newspapers Must Enter Social Stream to be on Trend." Retrieved from: www.issuu.com.

Al Thani, M. (2013). Jassim the Leader: Founder of Qatar. London: Profile Books.

Al Thani, T. (2015). "Qatar's Message to Obama." The New York Times. Retreived from: www.nytimes.com.

Al-Zayani, M. and Ayesh, M. (2006). "Arab Satellite Channels and Crisis Reports." International Communications Gazette, 68 (5-6).

Amara, M. (2013). "The Pillars of Qatar's International Sport Strat-egy." E-International Relations. Retrieved from: www.eir.info.

Amnesty International. (2018). "Qatar: New Fund Could Bring Hope to Exploited Migrant Workers." Retrieved from: www.amnesty.org.

Anderson, N. (2015). "In Qatar's Education City, U.S. Colleges are Building an Academic Oasis." Retrieved from: www.washingtonpost.com.

Bibliography

Anscombe, F. (1997). "The Ottoman Gulf: The Creation of Kuwait, Saudi Arabia, and Qatar." New York: Columbia University Press.

Associated Press (2019). "Exxon, Qatar Petroleum to Expand Golden Pass LNG Export Plant in Sabine Pass." Channel 12 News. Retrieved from: www.12newsnow.com.

Aspire Zone Foundation (2021). "The Business of Sports Accelerated." Retrieved from: www.sportaccelerator.qa.

Attwood, E. (2016). "Revealed: Qatar's $400m-a-Year Bill to Host Six Top US Universities." Retrieved from: www.arabian-business.com.

Atwood, K. (2020). "DOJ Orders Al Jazeera Platform to Register as Foreign Agent." Retrieved from: www.cnn.com.

Apostolic Vicariate of Southern Arabia "AVOSA." (2014). "Fr. John Van Deerlin Passes Away." Retrieved from: www.avosa.org.

Bahri, L. (2001). "The New Arab Media Phenomenon: Al-Jazeera in Qatar." The Journal of Middle East Politics.

Bandler, A. (2019). "GOP Members of Congress Call on DOJ to designate Al Jazeera as Foreign Agent." Retrieved from: www.jewishjournal.com.

BBC News. (2011). "Souq Waqif, Doha's Resilient, Labyrinthine Market." Retrieved from: www.bbc.com.

Benmayor, G. (2012). "The Unavoidable Rise of Turkish Contractors Abroad." Retrieved from: www.hurriyetdailynews.com.

Brewer, D. et.al. (2007). "A New System for K-12 Education in Qatar." Retrieved from: www.rand.org.

Campagna, J. (2001). "Between Two Worlds." Committee to Protect Journalists. Retrieved from: www.cpj.org.

Casiraghi, L. (2008). "The Church of So Many Humble People." Retrieved from: www.30giorni.it.

Castelier, S. and Poure, C. (2018). "In Qatar, Christianity Grows on the Fringes." Retrieved from: www.english.alaraby.co.uk.

Chadwick, S. (2020). "The COVID-19 World Cup?" Asia & the Pacific Policy Society. Retrieved from: www.policyforum.net.

Chan, S. (2016). "Sheikh Khalifa Bin Hamad Al Thani, Former Emir of Qatar, Dies at 84." Retrieved from: www.nytimes.com.

CIA World Factbook. (2020). "The World Factbook – Qatar." Retrieved from: cia.gov.

CNN Network. (2005). "Qatar Offers $100m to Relief Fund." Retrieved from: www.cnn.com.

Bibliography

Cole, A. (2019). "Review: Jean Nouvel's National Museum of Qatar Opens With Surprises at Every Turn." Retrieved from: www.theartnewspaper.com.

Come, T. & Raspaud, M. (2018). "Sports Diplomacy: A Strategic Challenge for Qatar." Hermes, La Revue. Retrieved from: www.cairnint.info.

Commins, D. (2012). The Gulf States: A Modern History. London: I.B. Tauris.

Constantine, T. (2019). "Qatar Airways: Simply the Best." Retrieved from: www.washington-times.com.

Conway, E. (2007). "Britain Has Slashed its Reliance on Mideast Oil." Retrieved from: www.telegraph.co.uk.

Cooper, R. (2017). "Another Qatari Firm Makes D.C. Hotel Buy." Washington Business Journal. Retrieved from: www.bizjournals.com.

Cords, S. (2019). "Qatar's New National Museum: Inspired by the Desert Rose." Deutsche Welle. Retrieved from: www.dw.com.

Council on Foreign Relations (2017). "Oil Dependence and U.S. Foreign Policy 1850-2017." Retrieved from: www.cfr.org.

Cronk, T. (2018). "Mattis, Tillerson Co-Host First U.S.-Qatar Strategic Dialogue." Department of Defense News. Retrieved from: www.defense.gov.

Crow, K. (2008). "Art's New Oasis." Retrieved from: www.wsj.com

Crystal, J. (1990). Oil and Politics in the Gulf: Rulers and Merchants in Kuwait and Qatar. Cambridge: Cambridge University Press.

D'mello, C. (2015). "Qatar's MIA, Mathaf Shortlisted for Museum 'Oscar' Awards." Retrieved from: dohanews.com.

Day, B. (2020). "L.A. Mayor Announces Expansion of Angeleno Card Program After Qatar Gifts $5 Million." Retrieved from: www.ktla.com.

Daye, A. (2018). "Qatar Looks to Take Lead in U.S. Real Estate Investments By Gulf Wealth Funds." Cornell Real Estate Review. Retrieved from: www.blog.realestate.cornell.edu.

Debre, I. (2020). "Qatar's Emir Promises Shura Council Elections Next Year." Retrieved from:www.apnews.com.

Dennis, E., Martin, J., & Wood, R. (2017). "Media Use in the Middle East: A Seven-Nation Survey." Northwestern University of Qatar. Retrieved from: www.mideastmedia.org.

Diba, B. (2014). "Is Qatar Plundering Iran's Share in the South Pars Joint Gas Field?" Retrieved from: www.payvand.com

El-Nawawy, M. & Iskandar, I. (2002). Al-Jazeera: How the Free Arab News Network Scooped the World and Changed the Middle East. Philadelphia, PA: Westview Press.

Bibliography

Embassy of Qatar (2020). "Philanthropy Framework." Qatar Embassy in Washington - USA. Retrieved from: www.washington.embassy.qa.

Embassy of Qatar. (2020). "The State of Qatar Donates $1 Million to Six Organizations in Florida to Help Counter the Repercussions of the Coronavirus." Embassy of the State of Qatar in Washington.

EuroPetrole. (2017). Qatar Petroleum and ExxonMobil Sign Exploration and Production Sharing Contract with Cyprus." Retrieved from: www.euro-petrole.com.

Exell, K. & Rico, T. (2013). "There is No Heritage in Qatar: Ori- entalism, Colonialism and Other Problematic Histories." World Archaeology. Retrieved from: www.tandfonline.com.

Fadlelmula, F. & Koc, M. (2016). Overall Review of Education System in Qatar. Germany: Lambert Academic Publishing.

Finkelstein, A. (2011). "Qatar Enters U.S. Market with Deal to Help Fund $700 Million D.C. City Center Project." The World Property Journal. Retrieved from: www.worldpropertyjournal.com.

Finn, T. (2015). "Qatar Slavery Museum Aims to Address Modern Exploitation." Retrieved from: www.reuters.com.

Fisher, M. (2017). "Qatar is Suddenly Investing in the U.S., Bankrolling D.C.'s City Center, Other Projects." Retrieved from: www.washingtonpost.com.

Folkenflik, D. (2011). "Clinton Lauds Virtues of Al Jazeera: 'It's Real News.'" National Public Radio. Retrieved from: www.npr.org.

France24. (2019). "Nouvel's Desert Rose Finally Blooms as Qatar In-augurates National Museum." Retrieved from: www.france24.com.

Fromherz, A. (2012). Qatar: A Modern History. London: I.B. Tauris.

Goff, K. (2017). "D.C. Going After Mideast Money for Devel- opment Projects." Washington Business Journal. Retrieved from: www.bizjournals.com.

Grynbaum, M., IIsu, T., and Robertson, K. (2021). "How News Organizations Got Afghan Colleagues Out of Kabul." Retrieved from: www.nytimes.com.

Hasaj, G. (2020). "U.S. Natural Gas: Once Full of Promise, Now in Retreat." Council on Foreign Relations. Retrieved from: www.cfr.org.

Hashimoto, K. et. al. (2004). "Liquefied Natural Gas From Qa-tar: The Qatargas Project." Baker Institute for Public Policy at Rice University. Retrieved from: www.bakerinstitute.org.

Heard-Bey, F. (2008). From Tribe to State: The Transformation of Political Structure in Five States of the GCC. Milan: Universita Cattolica del Sacro Cuore.

Bibliography

Henderson, S. (2000). "The 'Al-Jazeera Effect." Washington Insti- tute for Near East Policy. Retrieved from: www.washingtoninstitute.org.

Hill, L. (2019). "Inside the New, Architecturally Impressive National Museum of Qatar." Retrieved from: www.forbes.com

Hounshell, B. (2012). "The Qatar Bubble." Retrieved from: foreignpolicy.com.

Government of Qatar "Hukoomi." (2020). "Aspire Zone - Delivering on the Sporting Aspirations of a Nation." Retrieved from: www.gov.qa.

Gulf Times Newspaper. (2019). "Media City Entities to Enjoy Many Incentives." Retrieved from: www.gulf-times.com.

Human Rights Watch. (2018). "Qatar: Gulf's First Refugee Asylum Law." Retrieved from: www.hrw.org.

International Labour Organization "ILO." (2019). "Assessment of the Wage Protection System in Qatar." Retrieved from: www.ilo.org.

International Labour Organization "ILO." (2019). "Landmark Labour Reforms Signal End of Kafala System in Qatar." Retrieved from: www.ilo.org.

International Trade Administration (2020). "Employment and Trade." United States Department of Commerce. Retrieved from: www.legacy.trade.gov.

Ismail, I. (2004). Arab Daily Press in Qatar. Doha: National Council for Culture, Arts and Heritage.

Kanady, S. (2018). "Dr. Ibrahim Unravels History of Qatar's Gas Story at CMU-Qatar." Retrieved from: www.thepeninsulaqatar.com.

Katara. (2020). "About Katara." Katara Cultural Village Foundation. Retrieved from: www.katara.net

Katzman, K. (2019). "Qatar: Governance, Security, and U.S. Policy." Congressional Research Service. Retrieved from: https://sgp.fas.org.

Kayahan, A. (2014). "Unseen Treasures of Islamic Art Found in Doha." Retrieved from: www.dailysabah.com

Kennedy, C. (2002). "Foreign Affairs Oral History Project: Am- bassador Patrick Theros." Association for Diplomatic Studies and Training.

Khan, T. (2016). "Doha Slavery Museum Confronts Past to Help Qataris Shape Future." Retrieved from: www.thenational.ae.

Knecht, E. (2019). "Qatar Investment Authority aims to reach $45 billion in U.S. investments: CEO." Retrieved from: www.reuters. com.

Kobaisi, A. (1979). "The Development of Education in Qatar, 1950- 1977 With an Analysis of Some Educational Problems." Thesis, Durham University.

Bibliography

Koranteng, J. (1999). "Rivals, Youth, Force MBC to Alter Image." Advertising Age International.

Krane, J. (2005). "In Qatar, 1st Church Since 7th Century." Retrieved from: www.washingtonpost.com.

Krouse, S. (2011). "Qatar Fund Starts CityCenter Project With $700m Investment." Washington Business Journal. Retrieved from: www.bijournals.com.

Light, J. (2019). "Al Jazeera Target of UAE Campaign in US to Hobble Network." Retrieved from: www.bloomberg.com.

Linaker, E. (2014). "Qatari Entrepreneurship on Social Media." Retrieved from: www.ogilvyasia.com.

Lipton, E. et. al. (2018). "Foreign Powers Buy Influence at Think Tanks." Retrieved from: www.nytimes.com.

Lorimer, J. G. (1915). Gazetteer of the Persian Gulf, Oman and Central Arabia. India: Superintendent Government Printing.

Lynch, M. (2014). The Arab Uprisings Explained: New Contentious Politics in the Middle East. Columbia University Press.

Maj (2013). "Qatar Sports Diplomacy and Soft Power." Public Diplomacy and Global Communication Blog. Retrieved from: www.pdgc2013b.wordpress.com.

McKinsey & Company (2020). "The Future of Liquefied Natural Gas: Opportu-nities for Growth." Retrieved from: www. mckinsey.com.

MENA Financial News "MENAFN" (2019). "Qatar - Central Municipal Council Election: Voting on Tuesday." Retrieved from: www.menafn.com.

Metz, H. (1988). "The Turkish Petroleum Company." Washington D.C.: Library of Congress, Federal Research Division.

Metz, H. (1994). "Persian Gulf States: Country Studies." Washington D.C.: Library of Congress, Federal Research Division.

Middle East Monitor (2020). "New York Governor Thanks Qatar for Medical Aid to Fight Coronavirus." Retrieved from: www.middleeastmonitor.com.

Middle East Monitor (2020). "Qatar to Teach Human Rights in Schools." Retrieved from: www.middleeastmonitor.com

Morton, M. (2017). "Empires and Anarchies: A History of Oil in the Middle East." London: Reaktion Books.

Mourtada, R., & Salem, F. (2012). "Social Media, Employment and Entrepreneurship: New Frontiers for the Economic Empowerment of Arab Youth?" Dubai School of Governance. Retrieved from: www.researchgate.net.

Murray, B. (2017). "Hines, Qatari Team Up on CityCenterDC Hotel."

Bibliography

Commercial Property Executive. Retrieved from: www.cpexecutive.com.

Nasser, R. (2017). "Qatar's Educational Reform Past and Future: Challenges in Teacher Development." Open Review of Educational Research. Retrieved from: www.tandfonline.com.

Mourtada, R., & Salem, F. (2012). "Social Media, Employment and Entrepreneurship: New Frontiers for the Economic Empowerment of Arab Youth?" Dubai School of Governance. Retrieved from: www.researchgate.net.

Murray, B. (2017). "Hines, Qatari Team Up on CityCenterDC Hotel." Commercial Property Executive. Retrieved from: www.cpexecutive.com.

Nasser, R. (2017). "Qatar's Educational Reform Past and Future: Challenges in Teacher Development." Open Review of Educational Research. Retrieved from: www.tandfonline.com.

Neibauer, M. (2020). "Georgetown's Historic Hollerith House Sells in One of D.C.'s Most Expensive Deals." Washington Business Journal. Retrieved from: www.bizjournals.com.

Qatar National Human Rights Committee "NHRC." (2009). "Inauguration of United Nations Human Rights Centre in Doha." Retrieved from: www.nhrc-qa.org.

Office Holidays. (2020). "National Sports Day in Qatar in 2021." Retrieved from: www.officeholidays.com.

Office of the United States Trade Representative in Qatar. (2020). Retrieved from: www.ustr.gov.

Ouroussoff, N. (2008). "In Qatar, For I.M. Pei, History is Still Happening." Retrieved from: www.nytimes.com.

Oxford Business Group (2019). "Qatar's Position as International Sports Center Supprted by Investment, Partnerships." www.oxfordbusinessgroup.com.

Özbaran, S., & De Lyma, D. (1972). The Ottoman Turks and The Portuguese In The Persian Gulf, 1534 - 1581. Journal of Asian His- tory, 6(1), 45-87.

Pham, P. (2010. Ending "East of Suez": The British Decision to Withdraw from Malaysia and Singapore 1964-1968. London: Oxford University Press.

Phelan, J. (2014). "This is How These 12 Countries Will Punish You for Insulting Their Heads of State." Retrieved from: www.pri.org.

Pitts, M. (2016). "Beatrice de Cardi Obituary." Retrieved from: www.theguardian.com.

Pope, J. (2008). "N.O. Thanks Qatari Ruler for Support After Storm." Retrieved from: www.nola.com.

Bibliography

Potter, L. (2017. Society in the Persian Gulf, Before and After Oil. Qatar: Georgetown University Center for International Research and Regional Studies.

Qatar America Institute. (2020). "Qatar-America Relations." Retrieved from: www.qataramerica.org.

Qatar Digital Library. (2020). "21/5 Qatar Hospital." Retrieved from: www.qdl.qa.

Qatar Digital Library. (2020). "India Office Records and Private Papers." Retrieved from: www.qdl.qa.

Qatar Foundation. (2020). "About Qatar Foundation." Retrieved from: www.qf.org.qa.

Qatar Foundation International. (2020). "Snapshots of Our Work." Retrieved from: www.qfi.org

Qatar National Human Rights Committee "NHRC". (2020. "4,275 rights violations by siege states: NHRC." Retrieved from: www.gulftimes.com.

Qatar Petroleum. (2019). "Qatar Petroleum and Chevron Phillips Chemical Sign Agreement for a Mega-Petrochemical Plant in the United States." Retrieved from: www.qp.com.qa.

Qatar Tourism Authority. (2019). "Pearl Diving in Qatar." Retrieved from: www.qittour.com.

Rahman, H. (2006). The Emergence Of Qatar. Routledge.

RAND Corporation (2020). "Rand-Qatar Policy Institute." Retrieved from: www.rand.org.

Reiche, D. (2014). "Investing in Sporting Success as a Domestic and Foreign Policy Tool: the Case of Qatar." Retrieved from: www.belfercenter.org.

Reuters (2021). "Qatar and Turkey Working to Restore Kabul Passenger Flights." Retrieved from: www.reuters.com

Reuters Staff. (2019). "Exxon Mobil Wins Three Exploration Blocks Offshore Argentina." Retrieved from: www.reuters.com.

Reuters Staff. (2019). "Qatar Investment Authority, Douglass Em- mett acquire $365 mln California real estate complex." Retrieved from: www.reuters.com.

Riedel, B. (2019). "Beirut 1958: America's Origin Story in the Mid- dle East." Retrieved from: www.brookings.edu.

Roberts, D. (2017). "Qatar: Securing the Global Ambitions of a City-State." London: Hurst.

Rosiak, L. (2018). "Elite Universities Hide Information on Funding From Ultraconservative Nation of Qatar." Retrieved from: dailycaller.com.

Bibliography

Ross, W. (2020). "Remarks by Commerce Secretary Wilbur L. Ross at the U.S.-Qatar Strategic Dialogue." U.S. Department of Commerce. Retrieved from: www.commerce.gov.

Roy, A. (2020). "Qatar's National Sports Day: Qatar's Rise As a Sports Hub of the World." Retrieved from: www.sportsmonks. com.

Rugh, W. (2004). "Arab Mass Media: Newspapers, Radio, and Televi-sion in Arab Politics." London: Praeger.

Sampson, A. (1975). "The Seven Sisters: The Great Oil Companies and the World They Shaped." New York: Viking Press.

Sanders, B. (n.d.) "Sports as Public Diplomacy." Retrieved from: www.uscpublicdiplomacy.org.

Scott-Jackson, J., Scott-Jackson, W., Al Naimi, F., Tetlow, E., & Cras-sard, R. (2014). "The Stone Age of Qatar: New investigations, new finds; interim report (poster)." Proceedings of the Seminar for Arabian Studies, 44, 317-324.

Sen Nag, O. (2019). "The Culture of Qatar." Retrieved from: www.worldatlas.com.

Sergie, M. (2019). "Inside Qatar's Spectacular 'Desert Rose' Museum." Bloomberg. Retrieved from: www.bloomberg.com.

Shaker, M. (2005). Encyclopedia of the History of the Arab Gulf. Amman: Osama House for Publishing and Distribution.

Snoj, J. (2019). "Population of Qatar by Nationality - 2019 Report." Retrieved from: www.priyadsouza.com.

Sorkhabi, R. (2010). "The Qatar Oil Discoveries." GeoExPro Maga-zine. Retrieved from: www.geoexpro.com.

Strom, S. (2006). "Qatar Grants Millions in Aid to New Orleans." Retrieved from: www.nytimes.com.

Qatar Foundation International. (2020.) "Classroom-Ready Materials for Teaching the Arabic Language and About the Arab world." Retrieved from: www.resources.qfi.org.

The Cultural Village Foundation "Katara." (2012). "Pearl Diving in Qatar." Qatar: Katara Publishing House.

The Peninsula Newspaper. (2019). "NU-Q and GU-Q Offer Joint Course on 'Qatar in the Contemporary Muslim World." Retrieved from: www.thepeninsulaqatar.com.

The Peninsula Newspaper. (2019). "Qatar Petroleum Signs 5-Year Condensate Feedstock Deal With ExxonMobil in Singapore." Retrieved from: www.thepeninsulaqatar.com.

The Peninsula Newspaper. (2020). "Souq Waqif: The Story Behind Qatar's

Bibliography

Favourite Heritage Market." Retrieved from: www.thepeninsulaqatar.com.

The Peninsula Newspaper. (2020). "US-Qatar Business Council to Help Enhance Bilateral Economic Ties." Retrieved from: https:// www.thepeninsulaqatar.com.

The White House. (2021). "Readout of President Joe Biden's Call With Amir Tamim bin Hamad Al Thani of Qatar." Retrieved from: whitehouse.gov.

The Telegraph. (2018). "Step Back in Time and Visit Katara Cultural Village." Retrieved from: www.telegraph.co.uk.

U.S. Census Bureau (2020). "Trade in Goods With Qatar." Retrieved from: www.census.gov.

U.S. Department of State (1947). "Memorandum Prepared in the Department of State." Retrieved from: www.history.state.gov.

U.S. Department of State. (1969). "Memorandum from Peter Rod- man of the National Security Council Staff to the President's Assis- tant for National Security Affairs (Kissinger)." Retrieved from: www.2001-2009.state.gov.

U.S. Department of State. (1972). "Telegram from the Department of State to Secretary of State Rogers in Australia." Retried from: www.1861.history.state.gov.

U.S. Department of State (1988). "Foreign Relations of the United States, 1955-1957: Volume XIII: Near East: Jordan – Yemen." Retrieved from: www.history.state.gov.

U.S. Department of State (2015). "U.S.-Qatar Economic and Invest- ment Dialogue." Retrieved from: www.history.state.gov.

U.S. Department of State (2020). "Foreign Relations of the United States, 1947, the Near East and Africa, Volume V." Retrieved from: www.history.state.gov.

U.S. Department of State (2021). "Joint Statement on the U.S.- Qatar Strategic Dialogue." U.S. Department of State. Retrieved from: ww.state.gov.

U.S. House of Representatives. (1999). "H.Con.Res.35 - Congratulating the State of Qatar and its citizens on March 8, 1999." Retrieved from: www.congress.gov.

U.S. Senate. (1999). "S.Con.Res.14 A concurrent resolution congrat- ulating the state of Qatar and its citizens on March 8, 1999." Retrieved from: www.congress.gov.

U.S.-Qatar Business Council. (2020). "American Chamber of Com- merce in Qatar." Retrieved from: www.usqbc.org.

UK National Archives. (1972). "India Office and Successors: Political Residencies and Agencies, Persian Gulf: Correspondence and Papers." Retrieved from: www.nationalarchives.gov.uk.

Ulrichsen, K. (2015) "The Political Economy of Arab Gulf States." Baker Institute

Bibliography

for Public Policy at Rice University. Retrieved from: www.bakerinstitute.org.

Ulrichsen, K. (2016). "Gulf States in International Political Economy." London: Palgrave Macmillan.

United Nations Department of Economic and Social Affairs. (2019). "2019 Revision of World Population Prospects." Retrieved from: www.population.un.org.

United States Census Bureau (2020). "Foreign Trade - Trade in Goods With Qatar." Retrieved from: www.census.gov.

US-Qatar Business Council (2020). "USQBC in Action." US-Qatar Business Council. Retrieved from: www.usqbc.org.

Von Ochssee, T. (2007). "ExxonMobil and Qatar Petroleum: An Example of Successful IOC-NOC Cooperation." IGU Gas Market Integration Task Force. Retrieved from: www.iapg.org.ar.

Walker, L. (2016). "What You Need to Know About Msheireb Muse-ums in Qatar." Retrieved from: www.dohanews.co.

Warshaw, A. (2012). "Sarkozy Weighs In on Winter Qatar 2022 World Cup Debate." Retrieved from: www.insidethegames.com.

Wasserman, G. (2017). "The Doha Experiment: Arab Kingdom, Catholic College, Jewish Teacher." New York: SkyHorse Publishing.

Wilkinson, J. (1991). "Arabia's Frontiers: The Story of Britain's Boundary Drawing in the Desert." London: I. B. Tauris & Co Ltd.

Wintour, P. (2017). "Qatar Given 10 Days to Meet 13 Sweeping De- mands by Saudi Arabia." Retrieved from: www.theguardian.com.

World Bank. (2019). "Labor Force Participation Rate, Female (% of Female Population Ages 15+)." Retrieved from: www.data.worldbank.org.

Yeanos, C. (2019). "Bringing the Church to Qatar: The Efforts of Ambassador Patrick N. Theros." Retrieved from: www. thenationalherald.com.

Yergin, D. (1990). "The Prize: The Epic Quest for Oil, Money and Power." New York: Simon & Schuster.

Zahlan, R. (1979). "The Creation of Qatar." Britain: Croom Helm

Zahlan, R. (1979). "The Establishment of Qatar." USA: Barnes & Noble Books Press.

Zayani, M. (2005). "The Al-Jazeera Phenomenon: Critical Perspec- tives on New Arab Media." London: Pluto Press.

Zednik, R. (2002). "Inside Al Jazeera (Perspectives On War)." New York: Columbia Journalism Review.

About The Authors

Dr. Khalid Al-Jaber is Director of MENA Center in Washington D.C. Previously, he served as Editor-in-Chief of The Peninsula, Qatar's leading English language daily newspaper. Al-Jaber is a scholar of Arab and Gulf Studies, and his research focuses on political science, public diplomacy, international communications, and international relations. He has published scholarly works in several books and academic journals. Dr. Al-Jaber obtained his PhD from the UK and MA from the USA. He also holds a Postgraduate Diploma from Fordham University, Stanford University, and Georgetown University.

Ambassador Patrick Theros is a Strategic Adviser for Gulf International Forum. Previously, he held positions as Political Advisor to the Commander in Chief, Central Command; Deputy Chief of Mission and Political officer in Amman; Charge D'affaires and Deputy Chief of Mission in Abu Dhabi; Economic Counselor in Damascus; and U.S. Ambassador to the State of Qatar. In a career spanning almost 36 years, he also has served in diplomatic positions in Beirut, Managua, Dharan and Abu Dhabi, as well as in the Department of State. During that period, he earned four Superior Honor Awards. After retirement Ambassador Theros served as President of the U.S. Qatar Business Council from 2000-2017.